HOME REPAIR AND IMPROVEMENT

WALLS AND CEILINGS

HOME REPAIR AND IMPROVEMENT

WALLS AND CEILINGS

BY THE EDITORS OF TIME-LIFE BOOKS, ALEXANDRIA, VIRGINIA

The Consultants
Jeff Palumbo is a registered journeyman carpenter who has a home-building and remodeling business in northern Virginia. His interest in carpentry was sparked by his grandfather, a master carpenter with more than 50 years' experience. Mr. Palumbo teaches in the Fairfax County Adult Education Program.

Mark M. Steele is a professional home inspector in the Washington, D.C., area. He has developed and conducted training programs in home-ownership skills for first-time homeowners. He appears frequently on television and radio as an expert in home repair and consumer topics.

CONTENTS

Techniques for Repair and Resurfacing

Whether your house is of masonry or frame construction, the materials and procedures in this chapter will help you renew and repair walls and ceilings with a professional touch. Gypsum wallboard, finished with tape and joint compound, figures in virtually every process except minor repairs. When resurfacing an existing wall, the key to a perfect job is a carefully fitted framework that is plumb, square, and level.

Applying joint compound over corner bead →

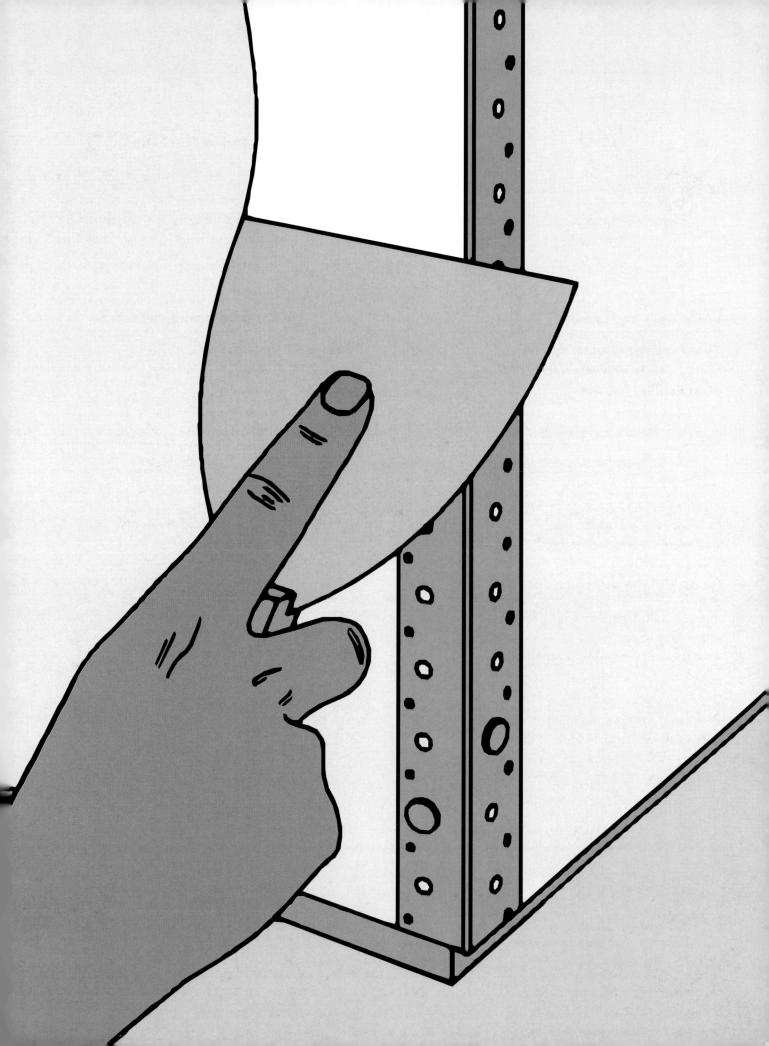

There's more to walls and ceilings than meets the eye. As the illustrations on the following pages show, the wallboard or plaster surface is nothing more than an attractive skin for the skeleton of a house.

Wood-Framed Construction: Of the four surface-and-structure combinations presented, wood-framed walls and ceilings covered by wallboard are the most common. The walls consist of vertical members, called studs, and horizontal members, the top plates and sole plates —all usually cut from 2-by-4 stock.

Larger boards called joists *(box, below)* define every ceiling and support the floor of any living space overhead; hence the terms "ceiling joist" and "floor joist" are often used interchangeably. The box describes several techniques for finding studs and joists in a finished wall or ceiling.

Masonry Walls: Older houses with exterior walls built of solid masonry are often finished inside with plaster laid on brick, but most such dwellings have ceilings and partition walls framed with wood joists and studs. Studs also lie behind the brick facades of many houses that are actually brick veneer, in which a single layer of brick is added to the outside of wood-framed walls.

Walls That Bear Weight: A wall that supports the roof or other upper structural parts of a house is known as a load-bearing wall, or bearing wall. In masonry houses, interior bearing walls are usually built of masonry. In a few frame houses, the studs of bearing walls are closer together than the standard 16-inch spacing for greater strength. Ceiling joists run perpendicular to bearing walls.

Finish Surfaces: Plaster over a bonding surface known as lath, most often made of wood or wire mesh, was once the most common wall surface. Wallboard made from gypsum sandwiched between heavy paper is now standard. Because wallboard requires neither lath nor drying time, it is more easily and quickly installed.

An attractive alternative to a plaster or wallboard surface is wood paneling, which is made of solid-wood boards or sheets of wood veneer. The paneling may cover the entire wall or just a portion of it as in wainscoting. Decorative molding conceals joints and provides a finished look to the room.

LOCATING CONCEALED STUDS AND JOISTS

For most wall and ceiling work, you need to know where studs and joists are. Typically they are 16 inches apart; finding one helps locate others. One way of detecting studs and joists is to tap the wall or ceiling, listening for the solid sound of wood behind wallboard or plaster.

Alternatively, check for visual clues to stud and joist locations. Examine wallboard close up for traces of seams or nailing patterns; this is best done at night with a light shining obliquely across the surface. If the work you plan requires removing the baseboard, look behind it for seams or nails that hold wallboard panels to studs.

The easiest approach is to use an electronic stud finder *(photograph)*, which indicates changes in structure density with a column of lights. As the tool is guided across wallboard or plaster, the lights turn on sequentially as it approaches a stud or joist. The top light glows when the stud finder reaches the edge of a framing member. You can approximate its center by finding the midpoint between the two edges.

No method is perfect. In each case small test holes drilled in an inconspicuous spot may be needed to pinpoint a stud or joist and to confirm the spacing between them.

WOOD FRAMING BEHIND THE SURFACE

Wallboard over studs and joists.
On this wood-framed wall, 4-by-8 panels of wallboard are secured horizontally with adhesive and nails or screws to vertical 2-by-4 studs. The studs are nailed between the sole plate (a horizontal 2-by-4 at floor level) and the top plate (doubled horizontal 2-by-4s at ceiling level). Studs are normally spaced at 16-inch intervals, center to center. Short pieces of 2-by-4 called firestops are sometimes nailed horizontally between studs at staggered levels to retard the spread of the flames in case of fire.

Alongside door and window openings, studs are doubled, and a heavy, beam-like assembly called a header forms the top of each opening. Short sections known as cripple studs extend above each header and below each window opening's rough sill, a 2-by-4 that runs across the bottom of the opening.

On the ceiling, wallboard covers 2-by-10 joists, 16 inches apart. Joist ends are toenailed to the upper surfaces of the top plates of two bearing walls.

Most pipes that run upward inside a

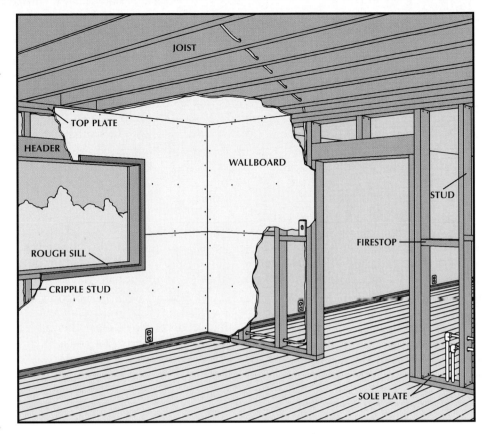

wall pass through the sole and top plates; holes in the centers of studs or joists—or notches cut in the edges—accommodate horizontal pipes. Vertical runs of electrical cable are stapled to the sides of the studs or joists; horizontal cables are threaded through $\frac{3}{4}$-inch holes.

DIFFERENT STYLES OF JOISTS

Instead of joists made of solid lumber like the ones illustrated above, your home may have one of the more modern kinds of joist shown here. Both types are stronger and lighter than lumber joists. I-beams (*below, left*) consist of two 2-by-4s joined by a plywood web. Open-web trusses (*below, right*) are built like bridge girders from 2-by-3s or 2-by-4s.

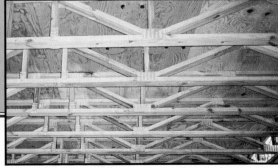

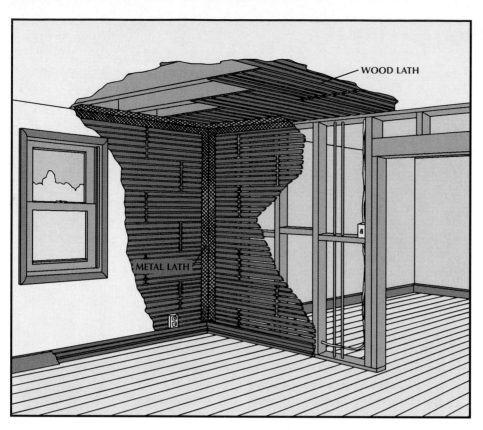

Plaster over wood lath.

The plaster finish that covers this wood-framed wall and ceiling is typical of house construction before 1930. The layout of wall studs and ceiling joists here is identical to modern frame construction *(page 9)*, except that spacing between the framing members varies from 12 to 24 inches.

A pattern of wood strips, called lath, anchors the plaster. Generally $\frac{5}{16}$ inch thick and $1\frac{1}{2}$ inches wide, the strips span up to four studs or joists, in staggered groups of four to six. The strips are spaced $\frac{1}{4}$ inch apart so that the plaster can ooze between them for a good grip. At corners, the wood lath is strengthened with a 4- to 6-inch-wide strip of metal lath.

MASONRY WALLS WITH WOOD-FRAMED CEILINGS

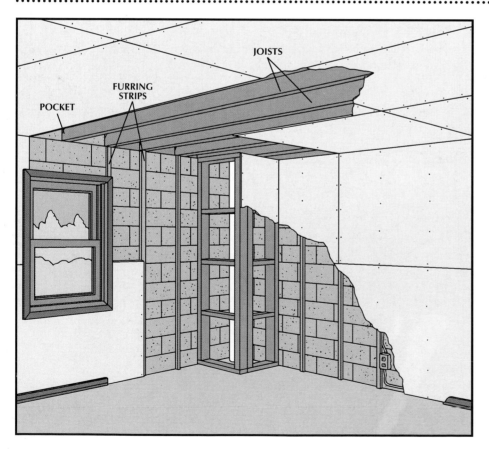

Furring strips under wallboard.

On a concrete-block wall, wallboard is nailed to vertical 1-by-3 wood strips, called furring strips. They are spaced at 16-inch intervals and secured to the blocks with masonry nails, adhesive, or a combination of the two. Enclosures built of 2-by-3s or 2-by-4s hide any exposed pipes.

On the ceiling, wallboard is attached to 2-by-10 ceiling joists whose ends rest in pockets made in the masonry walls at the time of construction.

Plaster over masonry walls.

In this masonry house, typical of the early 1900s, all exterior walls as well as interior bearing walls consist of two layers of brick separated by a narrow air space. Nonbearing interior walls are framed with wood studs. The ends of the ceiling joists rest in pockets that were made in the brick walls at the time of construction.

The plaster finish on the interior masonry walls is applied directly to the bricks; on walls and ceilings, the base underlying the plaster is wood lath, reinforced at corners with metal lath.

WOOD PANELING AND TRIM

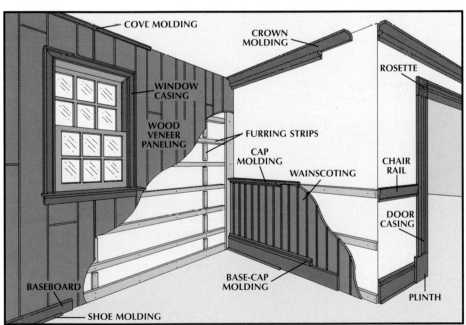

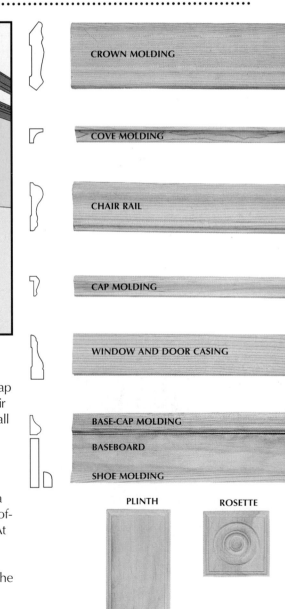

CROWN MOLDING

COVE MOLDING

CHAIR RAIL

CAP MOLDING

WINDOW AND DOOR CASING

BASE-CAP MOLDING

BASEBOARD

SHOE MOLDING

PLINTH   ROSETTE

Paneling over furring strips.

Sheets of wood veneer paneling may be attached directly to the wall or to a grid of furring strips as shown here. Grooves in the panel appear to be random but are actually placed every 16 or 24 inches to coincide with furring strips or studs. Decorative moldings and trim (photograph) smooth joints and provide finishing touches to the room. For example, where paneling meets the ceiling, cove molding, a convex wood trim, conceals the joint; baseboard and shoe molding cover the joint at the base of the wall.

Wainscoting is paneling that extends only partway up a wall. Attached and finished at the bottom like full-height paneling, wainscoting is topped with cap molding. Instead of wainscoting, a chair rail, originally created to protect the wall from furniture, may be set 36 inches from the floor.

Crown molding often trims the tops of walls. Made from a single molding or a combination of them, crown molding often detracts from fully paneled walls. At doorways, a plinth smooths the transition between the baseboard and door casing, and a rosette block decorates the upper corner of the doorway.

Repairs in Wallboard and Plaster

A wall or ceiling finished in plaster requires different repair techniques from one covered in wallboard, but the materials used are the same for both surfaces. For example, small defects in either kind of wall are filled with ready-mix vinyl spackling compound or joint compound, and large holes patched with wallboard.

Repairing Wallboard: It is not uncommon for dry-wall nails to pull away from the studs and joists and protrude. They are easily reseated and hidden with joint compound *(below)*. Corner beads may also need to be refastened to the wall and the corner reshaped *(opposite)*.

When patching anything much larger than a nail hole, you must first provide a foundation for the repair materi-al. Stuff holes up to an inch across with newspaper. Insert a wire screen for holes 1 to 6 inches wide *(page 14)*. And when large wallboard patches are needed, add braces for holes 6 to 12 inches across *(pages 14-15)* and cleats for those more than a foot wide *(pages 15-17)*.

Fixing Plaster Walls: To repair cracks and small holes in plaster, you must clear away the damaged material, fill the opening with joint compound, and sand the area flush with the wall. Undercutting the holes will allow the compound to bond better *(page 17)*. Large holes can be repaired with wallboard, but particular care must be taken not to damage the surrounding plaster *(pages 18-19)*.

 TOOLS

Nail set	Keyhole saw
Hammer	Electric drill
Putty knives	Dry-wall knives
Sanding block	Electronic stud
Metal file	finder
Utility knife	Chalk line
Carpenter's square	Cold chisel
Wallboard saw	

 MATERIALS

Wallboard	1 x 3s, 2 x 4s
Dry-wall screws (1",	Joint tape (paper or
$1\frac{1}{4}$", $1\frac{5}{8}$")	fiberglass)
Joint compound	Wood screws (3")
Sandpaper (coarse	Plaster washers
and fine)	Plywood ($\frac{1}{4}$")
Wire screening	Construction
Patching plaster	adhesive

 SAFETY TIPS

Protect your eyes with goggles when hammering, drilling, and sawing and when chipping away plaster. A hard hat guards your head from falling material when you are working overhead, and a dust mask protects your lungs when you are sanding and demolishing plaster.

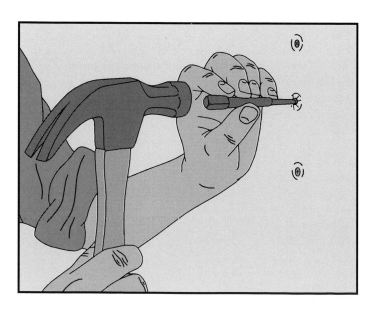

Hiding a popped nail.
◆ Install $1\frac{1}{4}$-inch dry-wall screws about 2 inches above and below the popped nail, dimpling the wallboard surface without breaking it.
◆ With a nail set and hammer, sink the nail about $\frac{1}{16}$ inch below the wallboard surface *(left)*.
◆ To check that the nail- and screwheads are countersunk properly, run a putty knife over them; a clicking sound indicates that they need to be driven in farther.
◆ Cover the nail and the screws with joint compound and let it dry.
◆ Apply a second coat of compound over a slightly larger area, let it dry, then sand with fine-grit sandpaper.

CAUTION

Safety Measures for Lead and Asbestos

Lead and asbestos, known health hazards, pervade houses constructed, remodeled, or redecorated before 1978. Test all painted surfaces for lead with a kit, available at hardware stores, or call your local health department or environmental protection office for other options. Asbestos was once a component of wallboard, joint compound, acoustic or decorative ceiling and wall materials, duct insulation, and heatproofing materials. Mist such materials with a soap solution of 1 teaspoon low-sudsing detergent per quart of water to suppress dust, then remove small samples for testing. Take them to a lab certified by the National Institute of Standards and Technology.

Wall and ceiling repairs where lead or asbestos is present require a tightly fitting respirator and protective clothing that's hot to wear. Hire a professional licensed in hazardous-substance removal if you suffer from cardiac or respiratory problems or don't tolerate heat well. And hire a professional for indoor jobs that require disturbing large areas of these materials.

When working around materials containing lead or asbestos proceed as follows:

! Keep children, pregnant women, and pets out of the work area at all times.

! Indoors, seal off the work area from the rest of the house with 6-mil polyethylene sheeting and duct tape, and turn off air conditioning and forced-air heating systems. Cover rugs and furniture that can't be removed with more sheeting and tape.

! Wear protective clothing (which is available from a safety-equipment supply house or paint store) and a dual-cartridge respirator with high efficiency particulate air (HEPA) filters.

! If you must use a power sander on paint containing lead, get one that is equipped with a HEPA-filter vacuum, but never sand asbestos-laden materials or cut them with power machinery. Instead, mist them with water and detergent, and remove them with a hand tool.

! Avoid tracking dust from the work area into other parts of the house, and take off protective clothing—including shoes—before leaving the work area. Shower and wash your hair immediately, and wash clothing separately.

! When you finish indoor work, mop the area twice, then run a vacuum cleaner equipped with a HEPA filter. Dispose of the materials as recommended by your local health department or environmental protection office.

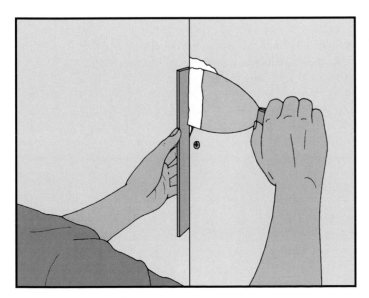

Rebuilding a corner.

◆ If the corner bead has been damaged, reseat it with $1\frac{5}{8}$-inch dry-wall screws and flatten any protruding bends with a metal file.

◆ Roughen the damaged surface on each side of the corner with coarse sandpaper, then brush clean and dampen.

◆ Holding a flat piece of wood against one side of the corner, apply joint compound to the other (left). Reverse sides and repeat, taking care not to dent the fresh joint compound.

◆ Scrape off excess compound and let the area dry for 24 hours.

◆ Repeat this step as required, using fine-grit sandpaper on a sanding block to smooth the patch after each coat.

FIXING SMALL HOLES IN WALLBOARD

1. Installing a backing.
◆ Pull out loose pieces of wallboard and cut away torn surface paper with a utility knife.
◆ Roughen the edges of the hole with coarse sandpaper and brush away the dust.
◆ Cut a piece of wire screening slightly larger than the hole and loop a string through the center.
◆ Tie a pencil to it, with 4 to 6 inches of slack *(near right)*.
◆ Wearing rubber gloves, coat the edges of the screen backing with patching plaster, roll the backing, and work it into the hole, maintaining a grip on the pencil *(far right)*.
◆ Reach into the hole, in order to dampen the edges of the wallboard,

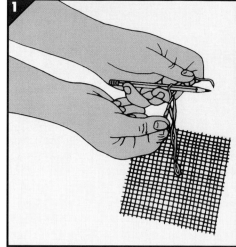
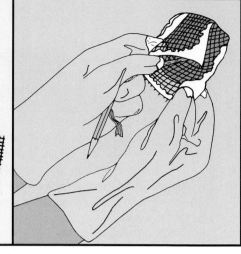

and then coat them with plaster.
◆ Carefully pull the backing flat against the hole.

◆ Wrap the string around the pencil, then twist it against the wall to hold the backing in place.

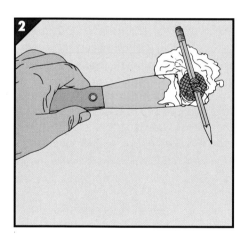

2. Applying the first coat.
◆ Using a 2-inch putty knife, gently fill the hole nearly flush with the wallboard surface, leaving a gap around the string *(left)*.
◆ Let the plaster set for 30 minutes.
◆ Cut the string as close to the screen as possible, freeing the pencil.
◆ Dampen the edges of the center gap, then fill it with fresh plaster.

◆ Fill the hole flush with the wallboard surface, then allow the patch to dry.
◆ Spread joint compound or spackling compound over the patch with a wide-blade putty knife. Make this top layer wider than the underlying patch.
◆ After the compound has dried for 24 hours, sand it with a fine-grit paper on a sanding block, feathering the patch's edges.

PATCHING EXTENSIVE DAMAGE

1. Cutting out the damage.
◆ With a carpenter's square, pencil a rectangle around the damaged area.
◆ Cut along the edges of the rectangle using a wallboard saw or a keyhole saw. With a wallboard saw *(right)*, start the cut by forcing the pointed tip of the saw blade through the wallboard. Drill holes at the corners for a keyhole saw.

As you saw around the damage, do not let the cutout drop behind the wall.
◆ Use the cutout as a pattern for a patch that is made from wallboard of the same thickness.
◆ From a 1-by-3, make two braces for the patch, each about 5 inches longer than the height of the opening in the wall.

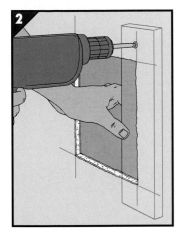

2. Installing the braces.

◆ Hold a 1-by-3 brace behind the wall so that it extends equally above and below the opening and is half hidden by the side of the opening.

◆ Drive a 1¼-inch dry-wall screw through the wall and into the brace, positioning the screw in line with the side of the hole and about 1 inch above it (left). Drive a second screw below the opening.

◆ For holes taller than 8 inches, drive an additional screw along the side.

◆ Install the second brace on the opposite side of the opening the same way

◆ Slip the wallboard patch into the opening, and screw it to the braces in the four corners and opposite any screws along the sides.

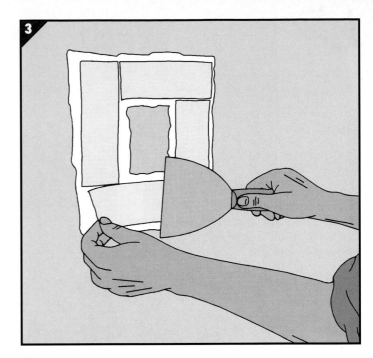

3. Taping the edges of the hole.

◆ Cover the screws and edges of the patch with joint compound, then embed strips of paper tape around the edges of the hole (above).

◆ Using an 8-inch dry-wall knife, stroke the surface of the joint compound from the center of the patch outward, tapering the edges of the patch to the level of the surrounding wall.

◆ Allow the patch to dry for 24 hours, then apply a second coat, feathering the edges.

◆ Once the patch has dried, smooth it with fine-grit sandpaper on a sanding block, feathering the edges.

SURGERY FOR LARGE HOLES IN WALLBOARD

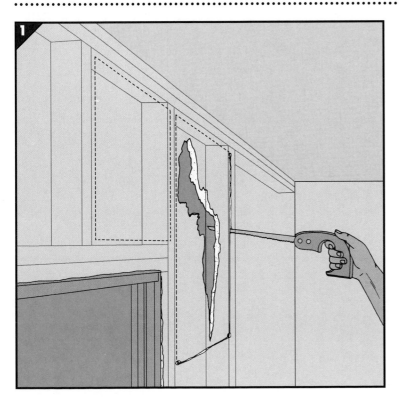

1. Cutting between studs and joists.

◆ Locate the position of the nearest stud or joist on each side of the hole (page 8).

◆ Using a carpenter's square, mark an opening with 90-degree corners to be cut around the hole. Draw along the inside edges of the two studs or joists that flank the hole, and along any framing members between them. If a stud frames a window or door as shown here, continue the marks to the next stud: Doing so avoids a joint in line with the opening, which would otherwise be subject to cracking from repeated opening and closing. Where a hole lies within 16 inches of an inside corner, draw to the end of the panel to avoid forming a new joint too close to the corner.

◆ Remove any wood trim within the marked-off area. If there are electrical fixtures or outlets, turn off power and unscrew cover plates.

◆ Cut out sections of wallboard between framing members with a wallboard saw or a keyhole saw (left).

2. Removing attached or blocked pieces.

Switch to a utility knife to remove wallboard attached to studs or joists or if you encounter obstructions in the wall (such as insulation or firestops).

◆ Cut through the sections, using a straightedge as a guide *(left)*.

◆ Take out any screws or nails and chip off any wallboard mounted with adhesive.

◆ Cut away joint tape and torn surface paper with the utility knife.

◆ At an inside corner, pull out pieces of wallboard wedged in the butted joint.

◆ Sand uneven edges around the opening with coarse sandpaper on a sanding block and brush debris from the exposed framing, cleaning it for the patch.

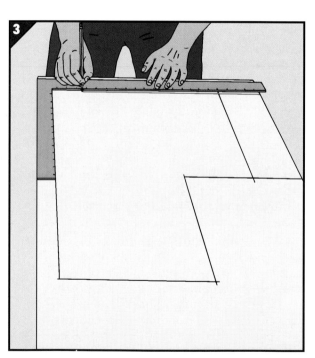

3. Making the patch.

◆ Measure each side of the opening as well as the sizes and positions of any electrical boxes, or door-frames or window frames, within it *(page 30)*.

◆ Transfer the measurements to a panel of the same type and thickness as the damaged wallboard, using a carpenter's square to ensure 90-degree corners *(above)*. Exclude the panel's tapered edges from the patch unless an edge of the opening falls at an inside corner.

◆ Cut out the patch, positioning the saw blade on the outline's inner edge; for an opening within the patch, cut just outside the line.

CLEAT · EXPOSED STUD · CLEAT

4. Adding cleats.

◆ For fastening the patch, cut 2-by-4 cleats to fit alongside the joists or studs at the edges of the opening. Where possible, cut the cleats 2 to 3 inches longer than the opening.

◆ Secure the cleats flush with the studs or joists using 3-inch wood screws driven every 4 to 6 inches along the cleat *(above)*.

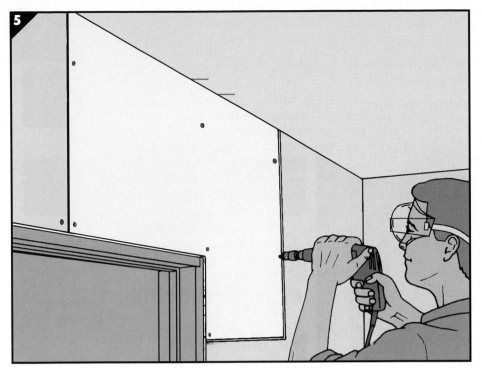

5. Installing the patch.

◆ Before positioning the patch, mark the location of any exposed stud or joist on the wall or ceiling near the opening.

◆ Fit the patch in the opening and drive $1\frac{5}{8}$-inch dry-wall screws through the patch about every 6 inches into each cleat, stud, or joist, starting at the middle and working to the edges *(left)*. Do not screw the patch to a top plate or a sole plate.

◆ Finish the repair as described in Step 3 on page 15.

FILLING CRACKS IN PLASTER

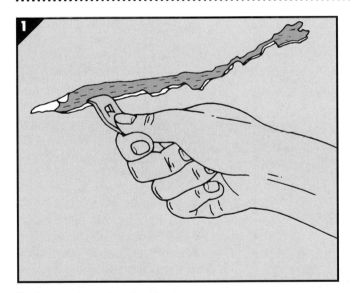

1. Preparing the crack.

This procedure applies to cracks comparable to the one shown here. Narrower cracks in sound walls do not require taping *(Step 3, overleaf)*.

◆ To help lock the patching material in place, scrape some of the plaster from behind the edges; a can opener works well *(above)*. Doing so makes the crack wider at the base than at the surface.

◆ Brush out dust and loose plaster, then dampen the interior surfaces of the crack.

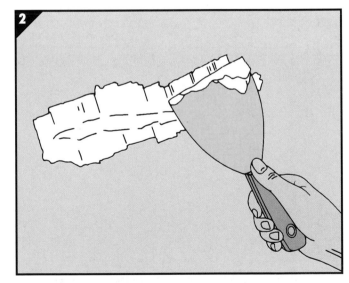

2. Filling the crack.

◆ Using a 5-inch dry-wall knife, pack joint compound into the crack, working it behind the undercut edges.

◆ Stroke the knife back and forth across the crack *(above)* until it is completely filled, then draw the knife along the crack to bring the patch surface flush with the wall.

◆ Allow the patch to dry for 24 hours.

3. Reinforcing the patch with tape.

◆ Cut a piece of fiberglass tape 2 inches longer than the crack.

◆ Spread a wide layer of joint compound over the crack.

◆ Press the tape into the compound, then run the knife blade along the tape to set it in place *(left)*.

◆ Allow the area to dry, then apply a second coat, feathering the edges.

◆ After the patch dries, sand it smooth.

WALLBOARD REPAIRS IN PLASTER

1. Removing the plaster.

◆ Snap a chalk line to form a rectangle that encompasses the damage.

◆ To protect sound plaster from damage while clearing deteriorated plaster from the rectangle, screw plaster washers just outside the chalked lines.

◆ Score the plaster along the chalked lines with a utility knife; then, with a hammer and cold chisel, remove the damaged plaster within the rectangle *(left)*.

⚠️ **CAUTION** *When chiseling plaster, work in small sections and tap the chisel gently. Excessive force can loosen plaster beyond the plaster washers.*

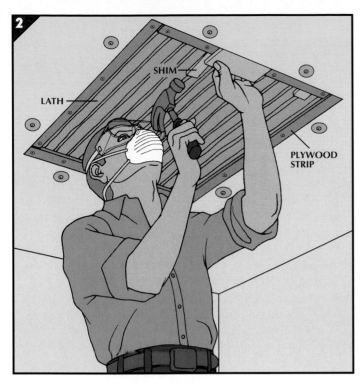

LATH

SHIM

PLYWOOD STRIP

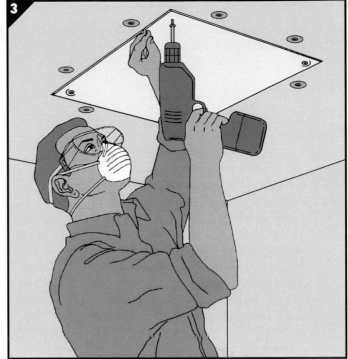

2. Attaching plywood strips.
◆ Cut strips of $\frac{1}{4}$-inch plywood, 1 inch wide.
◆ Edge each opening with the strips, loosely fastened with $1\frac{5}{8}$-inch dry-wall screws driven partway into the lath.
◆ Shim the strips to position a scrap of wallboard flush with the plaster *(above)*. Tighten the screws.
◆ Trim the protruding shims with a keyhole saw.

3. Installing the patch.
◆ Cut a piece of wallboard to fit the rectangle.
◆ Apply a bead of construction adhesive to each plywood strip, then press the wallboard against the adhesive.
◆ Fasten the wallboard to the plywood strips with 1-inch dry-wall screws 6 inches apart, starting at the corners *(above)*.

4. Taping the joints.
◆ With a 6-inch-wide dry-wall knife, spread a $\frac{1}{8}$-inch-thick layer of joint compound over all the joints *(left)*.
◆ Embed perforated-paper joint tape in the wet compound and run the knife over it, squeezing out excess material. Let the compound dry for 24 hours.
◆ Scrape off any ridges with the knife and apply a second layer of joint compound, called a block coat, with a 12-inch dry-wall knife centered on the joint. Allow the joint compound 24 hours to dry.
◆ Apply a final skim coat of compound with the 12-inch knife, feathering the material to a distance of 12 inches on both sides of the joint.
◆ When the compound is dry, smooth all the joints with fine-grit sandpaper.

When you refurbish a room with new wallboard or paneling, first-class results depend on a uniform underlying surface. If walls are not flat—without noticeable ridges and valleys—it will be difficult to apply the new covering satisfactorily.

Checking for Defects: A long, straight board will help you assess the condition of a wall or ceiling. Slide the board across the surface and look for gaps larger than $\frac{1}{4}$ inch between the two.

Small areas of imperfection can be rebuilt with plywood or wallboard patches, shimmed to bring them flush with the surrounding surface.

Redeeming a surface with more extensive flaws requires adding a grid of boards called furring strips or building a false wall in front of the old one.

A Furring-Strip Grid: Before laying out a grid for the strips *(opposite)*, remove moldings and trim, and adjust the depth of door and window jambs to suit the new wall thickness *(page 26)*. You may also have to reposition electrical outlet boxes or adjust their depth *(page 27)*. Plan vertical strips to coincide with the edges of the panels to be applied over them. In a wood-frame wall, nail the strips to studs where possible; between studs,

secure them using the method described on page 93.

Working over Masonry: Fasten the strips with case-hardened cut nails supplemented by construction adhesive. On any masonry wall below ground level, apply a coat of waterproof masonry sealer before attaching the furring strips.

If driving nails into masonry will compromise its watertightness, erect a false wall in front of it *(page 24)*. A false wall may also be needed if you plan new electrical junction boxes or switches, since the holes they require could create leaks in the masonry or violate local fire codes.

 TOOLS

Pry bar
Utility knife
Hammer
Nail set
Pin punch
Nail puller
Electronic stud
   finder
Carpenter's level
Straightedge
Chalk line
Plumb bob
Ladder
Tape measure
Saw
Framing square
Screwdrivers
Caulking gun

 MATERIALS

Furring strips (1 x 2
   and 1 x 4)
2 x 4s
2 x 4s (pressure-
   treated)
Finishing nails
Common nails
   ($3\frac{1}{4}$" and $3\frac{1}{2}$")
Wood shims
Construction
   adhesive
Acrylic latex caulk

 SAFETY TIPS

Goggles protect your eyes when you are driving nails.

PRYING OFF MOLDING AND TRIM

Removing a length of molding.
◆ If you plan to salvage shoe molding, cut the paint between the molding and the baseboard with a utility knife.
◆ Drive a thin pry bar into the seam near an end of the molding. Place a wood block behind the pry bar to protect the baseboard and slowly pry the molding loose.
◆ Work along the seam, using wedges to hold the seam open as you go *(above)*, until the whole length of molding is loose enough to remove in one piece.
◆ Apply the same technique to remove baseboards and other moldings.
◆ If you plan to reuse the molding, pull out the old nails from the rear with a nail puller to avoid splintering the face of the molding.

Removing window or door trim.

◆ To avoid splitting window or door casings as you pry them loose, use a pin punch to drive the existing nails completely through one section of each mitered corner, as shown here. A standard nail set is too thick for this task and will split the wood.

◆ Pry off the casing, using the technique described on the previous page.

A GRID OF FURRING STRIPS

A framework for plywood paneling.

Furring strips on this wall, backed by wood shims where needed *(page 23)*, make a flat base for vertical 4- by 8-foot sheets of wallboard or plywood paneling. Space horizontal 1-by-2 strips 16 inches apart from center to center. Place vertical 1-by-2 strips across the wall at 48-inch intervals, center to center.

Leave small gaps between vertical and horizontal furring strips to allow air to circulate behind the paneling. Place additional furring along corners and windows to support panel edges, and span the studs alongside an electrical outlet with a small 1-by-2. Horizontal 1-by-4 furring strips at the top and bottom of the wall serve as backing for cove and base moldings installed after the paneling is in place *(page 78)*.

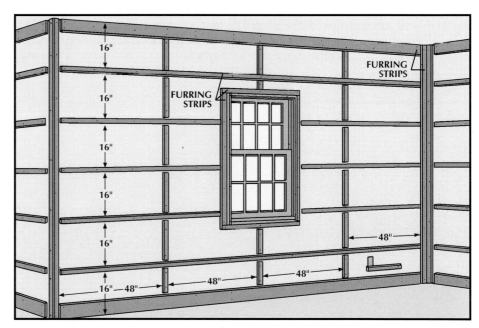

TRICKS OF THE TRADE

Fast Cuts with a Power Miter Saw

To speed the cutting of furring strips, consider renting a power miter saw, which slices through 1-by-2s with a single stroke. To minimize measuring, rent a model with an extension support on which you can set a stop block, then butt furring stock against the stop for cutting. The saw also pivots for angled cuts, making quick work of mitering moldings for a paneled wall *(page 94)*.

GUIDELINES AND SHIMS TO POSITION THE STRIPS

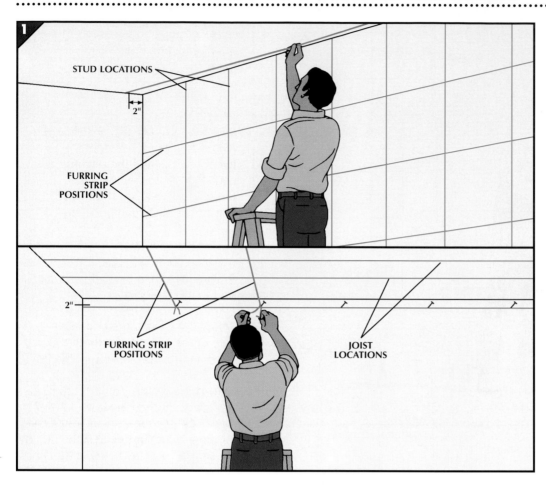

STUD LOCATIONS

2"

FURRING
STRIP
POSITIONS

2"

FURRING STRIP
POSITIONS

JOIST
LOCATIONS

1. Setting up reference lines.

◆ With a pencil and straightedge, rule the wall with vertical lines marking the locations of wall studs.
◆ In the same way, mark the horizontal positions where furring strips will be installed on the wall.
◆ Snap a chalk line against the ceiling, 2 inches from the wall *(left, top)*.

◆ On a ceiling, mark the locations of ceiling joists with a chalk line.
◆ Snap the chalk line 2 inches below the ceiling along the two walls that parallel the joists.
◆ Along each chalked line on the walls, drive nails every 16 inches for furring strips, and run taut strings across the joists between opposing nails *(left, bottom)*.

2. Positioning the first strips.

◆ Cut furring strips $3\frac{1}{2}$ inches shorter than the length of the wall or ceiling; make the top and bottom strips from 1-by-4s and the rest from 1-by-2s.
◆ For a wall, hang a plumb bob from the chalked line on the ceiling, opposite a line marking a stud.
◆ Measure the distance from the plumb line to the wall at each intersection of stud and furring strip line. Record each measurement on the wall.
◆ At the point with the smallest measurement—the highest spot along the wall—secure a horizontal, 1-by-2 furring strip with a single nail. Then nail the strip to the wall at any other line intersection marked with the smallest distance from the plumb line.

On a ceiling, use the same procedure to locate the lowest point, measuring from the joist lines vertically to the strings. Slip a furring strip under the string that crosses the lowest point and nail the strip to the ceiling wherever it crosses a joist line marked with the smallest ceiling-to-string distance.

3. Shimming the strip.

◆ At the first nail driven into the furring strip, hang a plumb bob from the chalked line on the ceiling and note the distance from the plumb line to the face of the furring strip.

◆ Reposition the plumb bob in front of the stud nearest one end of the furring strip.

◆ At the stud, place wood shims behind the strip until the distance between its face and the plumb line equals the measurement taken at the first nail. Drive a nail through the furring strip and shim into the stud. There is no need to glue or nail the portion of strip that extends from the stud toward the corner.

◆ Shim the other end of the furring strip in the same way.

On a ceiling, measure and make a note of the distance between the string and the furring strip at the first nail. Shim out one end of the furring strip until the distance from the string to the face of the furring strip is the same as at the first nailing point. Nail the strip to the joist nearest the end of the strip. Repeat at the opposite end.

4. Truing a furring strip.

◆ Press the edge of a long, straight board against the furring strip, spanning two nailed points.

◆ Note any gaps between the board and the furring strip or the strip and the wall, and build out these points with shims at each stud as you nail the furring strip in place.

On a ceiling, use the same technique to true and nail the first furring strip.

5. Installing the remaining strips.

◆ Install and true a 1-by-4 furring strip at the top of the wall and fasten it with two nails at each stud.

◆ Span the two trued furring strips with a long, straight board as an aid to fitting the remaining horizontal strips *(left)*, including the 1-by-4 strip at the base of the wall.

◆ At each corner, install two 1-by-2 vertical strips. Elsewhere on the wall, install vertical strips to fit between the horizontal ones and shim them flush with the horizontal strips. If a horizontal strip does not intersect a single high spot on the wall, shim the strip where it passes close to the wall and nail it there. Proceed as described in Steps 1 through 4.

On a ceiling, install and true two 1-by-4 strips along opposite edges, parallel to the reference strings and the same distance from them as the first strip, using the same techniques you employed on the wall. Install and shim a 1-by-2 under each string and at the two unfurred ceiling edges, with short cross strips where needed to support panel edges.

A FALSE WALL OVER MASONRY

1. Making the frame.

◆ For the top and sole plates of a false wall, cut two 2-by-4s the length of the wall. On a concrete floor, make the sole plate from pressure-treated lumber.

◆ Lay the plates side by side on the floor, with their ends aligned. With the aid of a square, mark the stud positions across both plates simultaneously, beginning flush with one end of the plates *(left)*.

◆ Mark additional stud positions at 16-inch intervals. Finish with marks for studs flush with the other end of the plates.

◆ Turn the plates on edge, the marked faces toward each other, and position 2-by-4 studs cut $4\frac{1}{8}$ inches shorter than the height of the ceiling or joists.

◆ Fasten each stud with two $3\frac{1}{4}$-inch nails driven through the plate and into the stud, top and bottom.

2. Erecting the framing.

◆ Raise the wall framing into position about an inch away from the masonry wall. Plumb the framing at several points with a carpenter's level.

◆ Cut strips of $\frac{1}{2}$-inch wallboard $4\frac{1}{2}$ inches wide. Insert them between the top plate and the ceiling or joists; push them into position against the masonry wall and flush with the edge of the plate, to act as firestops. Shim as necessary for a snug fit.

◆ Nail the bottom and top plates to the floor and the ceiling with $3\frac{1}{2}$-inch nails.

◆ In cases where panels will be installed horizontally, toenail 2-by-4 supports *(inset)* between studs at 24-inch intervals to provide additional nailing surfaces for the paneling.

◆ Install similar nailing surfaces around electrical boxes or access doors *(page 73).*

ENCLOSURES TO CONCEAL PIPES AND DUCTS

A vertical enclosure.

Most pipes, ducts, and girders can be enclosed with smaller, modified versions of a false stud wall *(above).* There is no need to add a dry-wall firestop above such a small enclosure.

◆ Construct two narrow vertical walls reinforced with horizontal supports.

◆ Nail the top plate of one wall to a ceiling joist; fasten the top plate of the adjoining wall to 2-by-4 blocking installed between joists.

◆ Nail adjoining end studs of the two walls together at the corner; secure the bottom plates of each wall to the floor.

◆ For three-sided enclosures, either vertical or horizontal *(page 26),* first construct and install two stud walls for the parallel sides of the enclosure. Then install horizontal supports to form the third side.

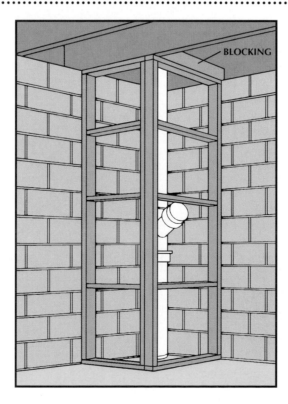

BLOCKING

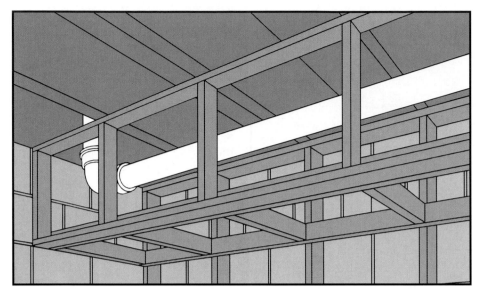

A horizontal enclosure.
◆ Construct two stud assemblies, one to be hung vertically from the ceiling and the other to fit horizontally between it and the adjacent wall *(left)*.
◆ Nail the vertical assembly through the top plate to ceiling joists or to horizontal blocking between them.
◆ Fasten the other assembly to wall studs, then nail together the top plates of the two assemblies.

DEEPENING WINDOW JAMBS

1. Removing a window stool.
To account for the additional thickness of a new wall surface and associated furring strips, add wood extensions to window jambs. Begin by removing the inner sill, called a stool.
◆ Drive all of the existing nails through the horn of the stool into the jamb *(page 21, top)*.
◆ Pry up the stool *(right)* and use it as a pattern for cutting a new one from stool stock *(inset)*, extending the back edge of the stool an amount equal to the thickness of the furring strips and new wall surface together.

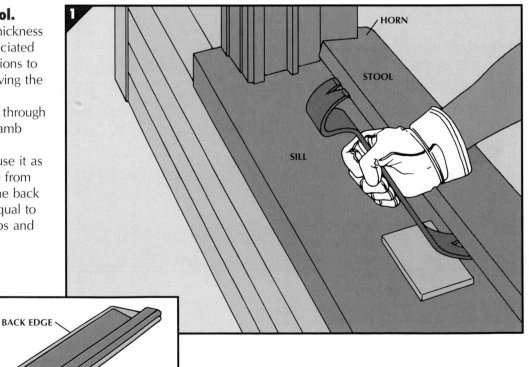

2. Attaching jamb extensions.

◆ From $\frac{3}{4}$-inch-thick stock, cut three jamb extensions—two for the sides, one for the top. Make the depth of the extensions equal to the combined thicknesses of the furring strips and the new wall surface.

◆ Nail the extensions to the edges of the jambs with finishing nails whose tips have been blunted to avoid splitting the thin wood, offsetting the extensions about $\frac{1}{8}$ inch from the face of the jamb (inset).

◆ Lay a bead of acrylic latex caulk in the corners formed by the extensions and the jambs.

If $\frac{1}{4}$-inch-thick paneling has been applied directly to a wall without furring strips, extend jambs with $\frac{1}{4}$- by $\frac{3}{4}$-inch lattice. This narrow stock lets you avoid the tricky job of sawing long, thin strips from wider boards.

STOPS

SASH

JAMB

CAULK

JAMB EXTENSION

EXTENDING AN ELECTRICAL OUTLET BOX

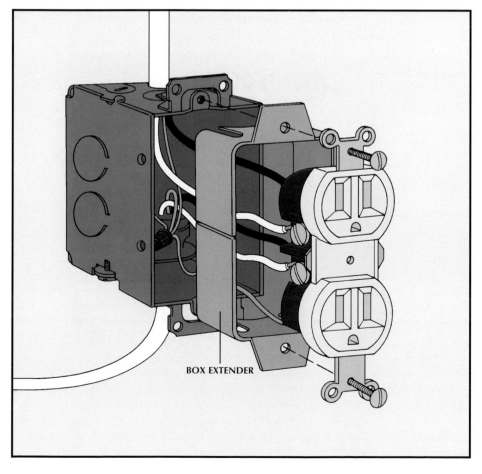

BOX EXTENDER

Attaching a box extender.

◆ Cut off the electricity at the main service panel and remove the fixture faceplate. Unscrew the fixture from the box, leaving the wires connected.

◆ Slide a collarlike extender over the fixture and its wiring and into the box.

◆ With the long bolts supplied with the extender, reattach the fixture to the box, adjusting the position of the extender so that the fixture will lie flush with the new wall surface.

New Surfaces Quickly with Wallboard

Wallboard, the material most commonly used to finish walls and ceilings, is simply a sheet of chalklike gypsum wrapped in heavy paper *(below)*. Easy to cut and somewhat flexible, wallboard can be fastened to a variety of supporting structures: joists, furring strips, or studs of wood or metal. The joints where panels meet are concealed with either adhesive-backed fiberglass mesh or paper tape and covered with pastelike joint compound *(pages 34-37)*.

Dimensions of Wallboard: Generally made in 4- and $4\frac{1}{2}$-foot widths, wallboard comes in 8-, 10-, and 12-foot lengths and in thicknesses of $\frac{3}{8}$, $\frac{1}{2}$, and $\frac{5}{8}$ inch; $\frac{1}{2}$-inch wallboard is considered standard. Using 12-foot sheets will save time, reducing the number of joints to be finished. But if such sheets are too heavy and unwieldy to handle, use shorter ones.

Before You Begin: To determine how many sheets of wallboard you need, calculate the square footage of each wall, ignoring all openings except the largest, such as archways or picture windows. Do the same for the ceiling. To convert this figure into sheets, divide it by the area of the panels you intend to buy. A 4- by 8-foot sheet is 32 square feet; a 4- by 12-foot sheet is 48 square feet.

Plan to hang panels horizontally rather than vertically on walls, unless the wall is very narrow. In rooms with ceilings higher than 8 feet, use sheets of wallboard $4\frac{1}{2}$ feet wide, trimmed to fit. If the ceiling is taller than 9 feet, you'll need a filler strip. Place it at the bottom of the wall, cut edge down.

You will also need fasteners—either nails or screws *(below)*—and adhesive, which reduces the number

of screws or nails required while greatly increasing the strength of the attachment.

Prior to hanging the panels, make sure the walls have sufficient insulation. If necessary, add insulating batts. Fasten them to the sides of the wall studs, with the vapor barrier facing into the room.

Hanging the Wallboard: Install the ceiling first, then the walls, always beginning in a corner. Measure and cut wallboard so that end-to-end joints fall at joists or studs and are staggered by at least 16 inches in adjacent rows.

Installing wallboard horizontally on walls results in fewer joints and fewer dips and bows. To further reduce the number of joints, wherever possible arrange wallboard sections so that joints fall along the frames of doors and windows.

 TOOLS

Dry-wall T square
Utility knife
Wallboard saw or
  keyhole saw

Tape measure
Chalk line
Caulking gun
Dry-wall hammer
Electronic stud
  finder

Screw gun or electric
  drill with screwdriver
  bit
Pry bar
Tin snips

 MATERIALS

Wallboard
Wallboard adhesive
Dry-wall nails or
  screws
Corner bead

 SAFETY TIPS

Protect your eyes with goggles when driving nails or screws.

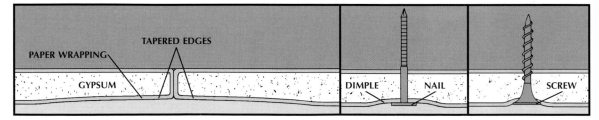

Wallboard and its fasteners.

The long edges of the wallboard panel are slightly tapered *(above, left)* starting 2 inches from the edge. When two sheets are butted side by side, they form a shallow trough for joint tape, making the seam easier to conceal.

Dry-wall nails *(above, center)* have broad heads and unusually sharp points. Buy nails with ringed shanks for extra grip

in wood framing or furring strips. Drive the nails to a depth slightly below the wallboard surface, and fill the resulting hammerhead dimple with joint compound. Neither the nailhead nor the dimple should break the paper wrapping.

Dry-wall screws *(above, right)* can be used in metal or wood framing. Sink screwheads to just below the wallboard surface, leaving the paper intact.

NAILS VERSUS SCREWS FOR HANGING WALLBOARD

A dry-wall hammer *(photograph)* is the tool of choice for nailing wallboard in place. It has a rounded head that reduces the risk of tearing the wallboard paper and leaves a dimple in the surface of the wallboard for easy filling. A sharpened edge opposite the head is useful for tucking excess paper on a trimmed edge into a joint for a neater seam.

But a misplaced hammer blow can damage wallboard, and nailing overhead is tiring, increasing the risk of error. Furthermore, a nail may eventually pop out of its dimple—espe-

cially on ceilings—if the wood in studs or furring strips is green.

For easier installation and a tighter attachment, use dry-wall screws. This thin, sharply pointed fastener requires no pilot hole and is easily driven through wallboard into either wooden or metal framing members with a screw gun *(below)* or an electric drill. A funnel-shaped head allows the screw to sink slightly below the wallboard surface without breaking the paper.

ELECTRIC MUSCLE FOR DRY-WALL SCREWS

If you decide to secure wallboard with dry-wall screws, you can use an electric drill equipped with a screwdriving bit, but a screw gun *(photograph)* will make the job easier. This tool has an adjustable depth gauge and a built-in clutch that stops the drill once the screw is driven the desired depth, greatly reducing the risk of tearing the wallboard's paper wrapping.

To set the depth gauge, rotate the collar on the nosepiece until the drill bit extends beyond the depth stop just enough for the screw to sink slightly below the wallboard surface. Test the setting by placing a screw on the end of the screwdriver bit. Then hold the screw gun to position the screw against the wallboard and squeeze the trigger while applying forward pressure. (The bit will not rotate unless pressure is applied.) When the depth gauge meets the wall, the clutch disengages and the bit stops rotating. If necessary, readjust the depth gauge to seat the screw properly.

DEPTH GAUGE   COLLAR

Shortening a panel.

◆ Position a dry-wall T square on a wallboard panel as shown at right and cut through the paper wrapping with a utility knife.

◆ Grasp the edge of the panel on both sides of the cut and snap the short section of wallboard away from you, breaking the panel along the cut.

◆ Cock the short section back slightly, then reach behind the panel with a utility knife to make a foot-long slit in the paper along the bend.

◆ Snap the short section forward to break it off.

DRY-WALL T SQUARE

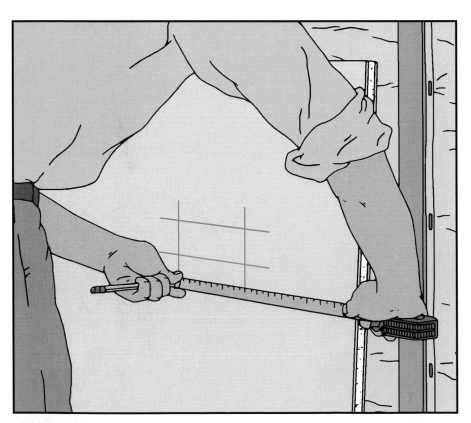

Making openings.

◆ To mark a panel for a small opening such as the hole for an electrical box, measure from the point on the wall where the edge of the sheet will rest to the near and far sides of the box.

◆ Similarly, measure from the point where the top or the bottom edge of the panel will fall to the top and bottom of the box.

◆ Transfer these measurements to the sheet: Hold the tape measure between your thumb and forefinger at the first measurement as shown at left. Rest the side of your forefinger against the edge of the panel and hold a pencil against the end of the tape with the other hand, then move both hands down the panel simultaneously to mark the first of the four edges of the opening.

◆ Repeat this procedure for each of the other three measurements.

◆ Cut the opening with a wallboard saw *(page 14)* or a keyhole saw.

For a larger opening, such as a window, mark the wallboard the same way. Cut all four sides with a saw, or saw three sides, then score and break the fourth.

HANGING A CEILING

1. Applying the adhesive.

◆ Measure and trim the first panel so the end not butted against the wall will coincide with the center of a joist edge.

◆ Mark joist locations on the panel with a chalk line.

◆ Apply a $\frac{3}{8}$-inch-thick bead of wallboard adhesive to the underside of each ceiling joist to be covered by the first panel. So adhesive will not ooze out between sheets, start and stop each bead about 6 inches from the point where the sides of the panel will fall.

◆ Also apply adhesive to the edges of the joists to which you will attach the ends of the panel.

2. Attaching the wallboard.

◆ With a helper or two, lift the panel into position against the adhesive-coated joists and drive a nail or screw into each joist at the center of the sheet. If using dry-wall nails, double-nail at each joist, except at the ends, driving a second nail 2 inches apart from the first.

◆ Fasten the tapered sides of the panel to each joist, 1 inch from the panel edges.

◆ Secure the ends with nails or screws spaced 16 inches apart and $\frac{1}{2}$ inch from the edge.

◆ Continue in this fashion until the entire ceiling is covered. If you find there will be a gap along the wall running parallel to the joists, trim panels to ensure that the filler strip *(page 32, Step 3)* will span at least two joists.

GIVING DRY WALL A LIFT

You can install wallboard without enlisting friends or neighbors as helpers by renting a dry-wall lift. This handy tool raises a wallboard panel to the desired height and holds it in position while you secure it to the wall or ceiling. Casters make the lift easy to position, and a brake keeps it from moving once it is in place.

To use the lift, rest one edge of a wallboard panel on a pair of metal hooks attached to a frame with adjustable arms that together form a cradle for the sheet. Angle the cradle for a ceiling or wall, then turn the wheel to raise the sheet of wallboard to the correct height.

Devising a Tapered Joint

The ends of wallboard panels, unlike the sides, are untapered. As a result, no shallow, joint-tape trough *(page 28)* is formed between sheets butted end to end, making the seam difficult to conceal. One remedy is to staple cardboard shims, $\frac{1}{16}$ inch thick, along the edges of the joists or studs on either side of the joint. The shims cause the wallboard to slope toward the joist or stud behind the joint, creating a slight depression for the joint tape.

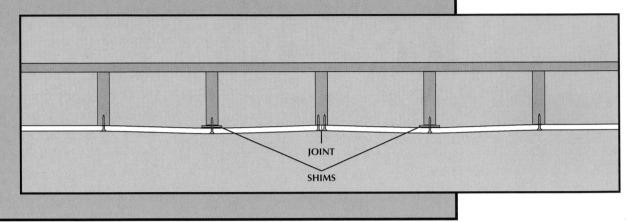

JOINT

SHIMS

FILLER STRIP

3. Adding a filler strip.

Fill gaps in the ceiling with wallboard strips cut to fit.
◆ Cut a strip from the side of a sheet and butt it against the adjoining panel so the tapered edges meet, ensuring a smooth joint.

◆ Secure the filler strip with adhesive and fasteners driven into the joists.
◆ Use a utility knife or the blade at the back of a drywall hammer *(page 29, photograph)* to trim away small amounts of excess gypsum.

SECURING WALL PANELS

1. Installing wallboard horizontally.

◆ On the ceiling and the floor, mark the centers of wall studs as a guide to fastening the sheets of wallboard.

◆ Trim the first panel to end at the center of a stud. Shim the adjacent studs if you choose (*opposite, top*).

◆ As for ceiling joists (*page 31, Step 1*), apply adhesive to the studs that will be covered by the first sheet.

◆ With a helper, lift the panel into place, tight against the ceiling. Secure it with three rows of fasteners driven into each stud an inch from the bottom edge of the panel, then across the middle, then an inch from the top edge. If using dry-wall nails, double-nail the midsection of the sheet (*page 31, Step 2*).

◆ Finish attaching the sheet with fasteners spaced every 8 inches across the ends, $\frac{1}{2}$ inch from the edge—except where an end falls at an inside corner. In that case, leave the end unfastened, butt the next panel against it, and fasten the end of the second sheet to a stud. At an outside corner, lap the end of the second sheet over the end of the first, and nail the ends of both panels to their common stud.

After the upper course, install a lower course, trimming the panels lengthwise to leave a $\frac{1}{2}$-inch gap at the floor. Arrange the panels so that joints in the lower course do not align with those in the upper one. With a helper, use foot levers (*Step 2, below*) to raise the panel off the floor while securing it.

2. Installing vertical panels.
For narrow sections of wall, install panels vertically, joining them at the midpoint of studs.

◆ Apply adhesive in the pattern for horizontal panels. Lift the panel into place against the ceiling, using a pry bar on a scrap of wood as a foot lever.

◆ Secure the panel to each stud with fasteners spaced about 2 feet apart, starting 1 inch from the top and ending 1 inch from the bottom. If using dry-wall nails, double-nail the midsection (*Step 1, above*).

3. Attaching a corner bead.
◆ To protect an outside corner, trim a metal corner-bead strip to the correct length by cutting through the flanges with tin snips, one flange at a time.

◆ Position the corner bead over the wallboard joint and fasten it to the stud beneath with nails or screws driven through holes in the bead.

The Art of Applying Joint Compound

All that remains after installing wallboard *(pages 28-33)* is to conceal fastener heads, corner bead, and the seams between dry-wall sheets. Joint compound is an essential element in all three tasks. Buy a 5-gallon drum of joint compound for every ten 4- by 8-foot sheets of wallboard you have installed.

Taping and Feathering: Covering fastener heads and corner bead requires only the application of joint compound. To hide and strengthen a seam between wallboard sheets, however, precede the joint compound with joint tape made of paper or fiberglass mesh.

Paper joint tape is stuck to the wall with an underlying layer of joint compound *(opposite)*, whereas fiberglass tape has an adhesive backing to make the work go more quickly. Either tape is then covered with two layers of compound in a process known as feathering *(page 37)*.

A Final Smoothing: After joint compound dries, you must sand or sponge away grooves and ridges. Sand with 120-grit, open-coat paper wrapped around a sanding block; a sanding plate on a pole lets you reach high areas. A light back-and-forth motion works best except for rubbing down a high spot, where a circular motion is preferable.

Sponging avoids both the dust made by sanding and the risk of scratching the wallboard's paper surface. Saturate a wallboard sponge with water, wring it dry, then gently rub it across the joint compound with a smooth, sweeping motion.

 TOOLS

Wallboard knives
  (5", 8", 12")
Joint compound
  pan
Sanding plate
  and pole
Sandpaper (120-grit,
  open-coat)
Wallboard sponge
Corner trowel
Crown trowel

 **MATERIALS**

Joint compound
Wire coat hanger
Paper or fiberglass
  joint tape

 **SAFETY TIPS**

Goggles shield your eyes from dripping joint compound when you are working overhead. Always wear a dust mask when sanding joint compound.

HIDING FASTENERS AND CORNER BEAD

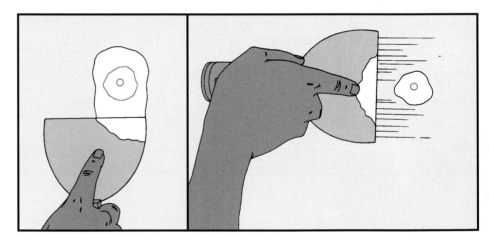

Covering a nail- or screwhead.
◆ Load half the width of a 5-inch knife blade with joint compound.
◆ Holding the blade nearly parallel to the wallboard, draw the compound across the nail- or screwhead so that it fills the dimple completely *(above, left)*.
◆ Raise the knife blade to a more upright position and scrape off excess compound with a stroke at right angles to the first *(above, right)*.
◆ Apply two additional coats in the same fashion, allowing the compound to dry between coats.
◆ After the third coat dries, lightly sand or sponge the patch smooth.

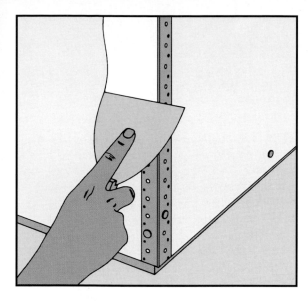

Covering a corner bead.

◆ Load the left two-thirds of a 5-inch knife with joint compound.
◆ With the right 2 inches of the knife overhanging the corner, run the knife down the left side of the bead (left).
◆ Load the right side of the knife and run it down the right side of the bead.
◆ Scrape the knife across the edge of a scrap of wood to clean it, then remove excess compound and smooth the joint by running the knife alternately down the left and right faces of the bead.
◆ Apply and smooth a second coat without letting the knife overhang the corner, feathering this layer about $1\frac{1}{2}$ inches beyond the first.
◆ Apply a third coat using an 8-inch knife to feather the compound an additional 2 inches on each side.
◆ Once the compound dries, sand or sponge it smooth.

APPLYING TAPE TO A FLAT JOINT

1. Applying joint compound.

When using fiberglass tape (photograph), skip this step and adapt the knife technique shown in Step 2 to stick the tape along the bare joint. A coathanger spindle, hooked to your belt, holds a roll of joint tape at the ready.
◆ Thin a batch of joint compound with a pint of water for every 5 gallons of compound, then load half the width of a 5-inch knife with the mix.
◆ Center the blade over the joint, cocking it slightly so the blade's loaded side is the leading edge, and smoothly run the knife along the joint (right). Hold the knife almost perpendicular to the wallboard at the start, but gradually angle it closer to the board as you draw it along the seam to fill the depression at the wallboard's tapered edges.

For an end-to-end joint, where the sheets do not have tapered edges, apply a $\frac{1}{8}$-inch-thick layer of compound.

SPINDLE

JOINT COMPOUND PAN

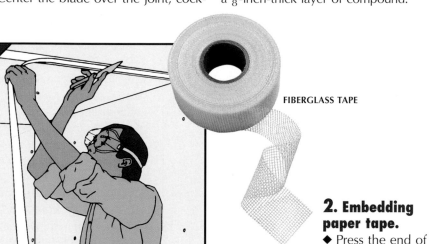

FIBERGLASS TAPE

2. Embedding paper tape.

◆ Press the end of the tape into the wet compound at one end of the joint.
◆ As you hold the tape over the joint with one hand, run the blade of a 5-inch knife along the joint with the other to force the tape into the compound (left). At the far end of the joint, use the knife as a straightedge in order to tear the tape.
◆ Run the knife along the joint a second time, pressing firmly to push the tape into the compound and to scrape off most of the excess compound.
◆ Then go over the tape a third time, pushing down on the knife to eliminate any air bubbles, and return the excess compound to the pan.

At an end-to-end joint, where the paper tape rides on the surface, do not scrape off excess compound completely. Leave a combined tape-and-compound thickness of about $\frac{1}{8}$ inch.

TAPING AN INSIDE CORNER

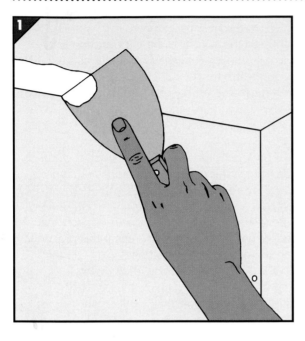

1. Applying the compound.
Fiberglass tape requires no initial application of compound; simply crease the
tape down the center and press it into
the corner. To apply paper tape:
◆ Load half the width of a 5-inch knife
with joint compound.
◆ Run the knife along one side of the
corner joint, then the other, lifting the
inside of the blade slightly to create a
thicker layer of compound at the joint.
Do not be concerned if you scrape off
some of the compound on the first side
while coating the second.

A corner trowel *(photograph)* has angled faces for applying joint compound
to both sides of a corner at once.

CORNER
TROWEL

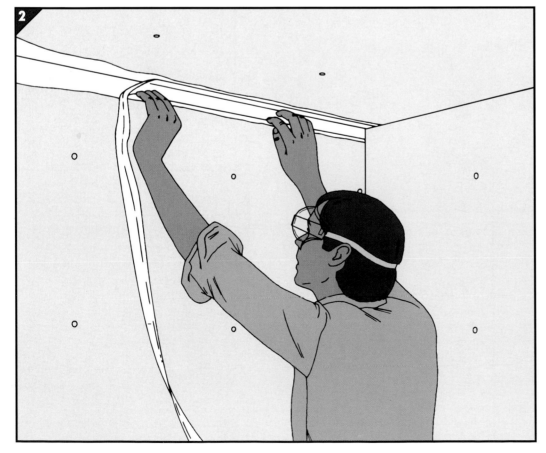

2. Embedding the tape.
◆ Fold the tape along its
lengthwise crease line and
press it lightly into the joint
compound with your fingers.
◆ Run a 5-inch knife or corner trowel lightly along both
sides of the crease, applying
just enough pressure to
make the tape stick to the
compound. Then repeat, using more force to squeeze
out excess compound.
◆ Finally, coat the tape
lightly with some of the excess, and run the knife or
trowel over it one last time,
leaving a film of compound
on the tape.

Completing a flat seam.
◆ For paper tape, thin the compound as described in Step 1 on page 35. With fiberglass tape, use the compound as it comes from the can.
◆ Load the full width of an 8-inch knife with joint compound and cover the tape with an even layer of the material.
◆ Clean the knife and draw it over this layer, holding the blade slightly off center and lifting the edge nearer the joint about $\frac{1}{8}$ inch. Do likewise on the other side of the joint to create a slight ridge that feathers out evenly on both sides.
◆ Let the compound dry and lightly sand or sponge it (page 34).
◆ For paper tape, thin the compound with a quart of water for every 5 gallons and apply a final layer with two passes of a 12-inch knife: On the first pass, rest one edge of the knife blade on the center ridge and bear down on the other edge; on the second pass, repeat this procedure on the other side of the ridge.
◆ Let the compound dry and give it a final sanding or sponging.

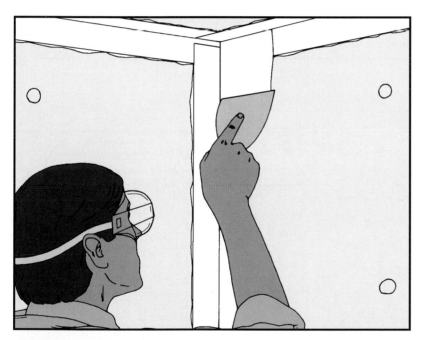

Feathering an inside corner.
For this procedure, thin the joint compound as you would for a flat seam (above).
◆ Load the full width of a 5-inch knife with joint compound and spread an even layer of compound over one side of the corner.
◆ Scrape off any compound that laps onto the corner's second side, then draw the knife down the first side again, bearing down on the outside edge of the knife in order to feather the compound.
◆ Smooth this layer one more time, removing any excess and scraping off any compound that was left on the wall beyond the feathered edge.
◆ After the first side of the corner has finished drying, apply joint compound to the second side in the same fashion.
◆ Then repeat this procedure on both sides with an 8-inch wallboard knife.

TRICKS OF THE TRADE

An Arched Trowel to Speed the Work

A tool called a crown trowel, or wallboard trowel, makes it easy to create a ridge in the joint compound over a flat seam. With a $\frac{1}{8}$-inch curve to the blade, it creates a ridge along the wallboard seam with a single swipe, instead of the two passes required with a flat 8-inch knife. After this ready-made ridge dries, sand or sponge it, then apply the last layer of joint compound with a 12-inch wallboard knife as described above.

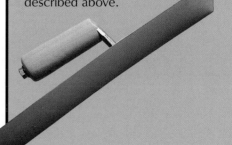

Decorative Moldings and Medallions

Artisans have been affixing molded decorations to walls and ceilings for hundreds of years. Such ornaments remain popular today, either to give authenticity to a restoration or to add interest to a flat surface. Lumberyards and hardware stores stock some styles, but many of the more elaborate patterns must be ordered from craft studios or manufacturers.

Ceilings and Walls: One common decoration is a medallion used as a backdrop for a chandelier or ceiling fan. It comes with a wiring hole that is covered by the fixture's ceiling plate. Since these plates vary in size, choose a medallion with a hole of the proper diameter.

Another popular trim is the molding used to frame the wall space above a fireplace, sometimes called a chimneypiece. The pattern must match precisely at the mitered corners, a goal that is easier to achieve with simple molding designs.

The Best Material: Ceiling and wall ornaments are made from plaster, wood, and plastic. Old moldings were generally cast in plaster; for a restoration project, you may prefer this material. Plastic, however, is lighter in weight and more durable than plaster; it makes a good choice for ceiling medallions. Wood is versatile as wall trim, for it can be either painted or stained.

 Before removing a chandelier, turn off the power at the service panel.

 TOOLS

Caulking gun
Tape measure
Carpenter's level
Chalk line
Miter box
Backsaw
Nail set

 **MATERIALS**

Wire caps
Panel adhesive
Wallboard screws or
    flat-head wood
    screws
Spackling compound
Latex caulk
Finishing nails (2")
Wood putty

ACCENTING A CHANDELIER

1. Marking the ceiling.
◆ After turning off power at the circuit breaker, disconnect the chandelier from its electrical box in the ceiling and cap the wire ends.
◆ Center the medallion over the electrical box using the hole in the crossbar of the box as a reference point. If the medallion design contains squares or rectangles, be sure they are parallel with the walls.
◆ Pencil a line around the medallion and mark the screw holes *(right)*. (If there are no screw holes, drill three $\frac{1}{8}$-inch holes, spaced evenly, near the medallion rim; then counterbore the holes so the screwheads will be hidden.)

38

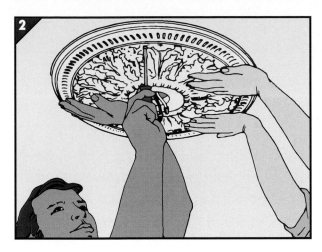

2. Attaching the medallion.

◆ Ring the back of the medallion with 2-inch-wide daubs of panel adhesive, spacing them so they are 2 inches apart.

◆ Press the medallion against the ceiling, aligning it carefully with the pencil marks.

◆ While a helper holds the medallion, screw it to the ceiling. Use dry-wall screws in wallboard, flat-head wood screws in plaster.

◆ Cover the screwheads with spackling compound and apply latex caulk around the medallion's rim.

◆ When the caulk is dry, paint the medallion, then rehang the chandelier and turn on the power.

A CHIMNEYPIECE ABOVE THE MANTEL

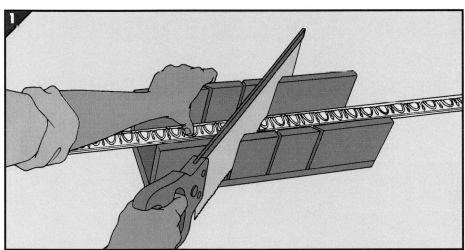

1. Mitering the molding.

◆ With a tape measure, carpenter's level, and chalk line, lay out a rectangle in the shape of the chimneypiece. Center the rectangle above the mantel; make the sides plumb and the top and bottom level.

◆ Transfer the dimensions of the rectangle to the molding strips to mark the locations of miter cuts. To make the design match neatly at the corners, you may need to alter the dimensions of the rectangle.

◆ With a miter box and backsaw, cut molding at a 45-degree angle for all four sides of the rectangle (left).

◆ Lay the strips on the floor to check the match at the corners. Trim the strips as needed, then daub panel adhesive on the backs of the strips at 1-foot intervals.

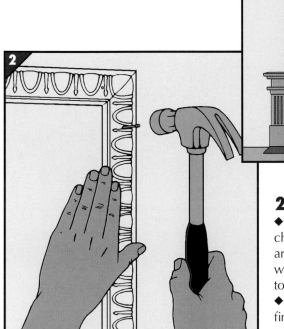

2. Positioning the strips.

◆ Place the molding on the chalked lines (inset). Where strips are not flush at a corner, place wood shims under the lower strip to make them so.

◆ Fasten the molding with 2-inch finishing nails, galvanized if the wall is plaster. Countersink the heads with a nail set.

◆ Fill nail holes and any gaps at the corners with spackling compound if the trim is plastic or plaster; use wood putty on wood trim to fill these areas or to conceal shims.

◆ If you plan to paint the molding, caulk the inside and outside edges.

Changing the Look of Rooms

2

The walls and ceilings that surround and protect us invite a variety of finish treatments. As alternatives to traditional paint and wallpaper, innovative options include lining walls with cork, brick veneer, and even mirrors. Painted brick walls can be restored to their original, textured beauty. And when the need arises, modern materials make it easy to transform a room with simple divider panels or whole new walls.

Tooling a mortar joint on a brick wall →

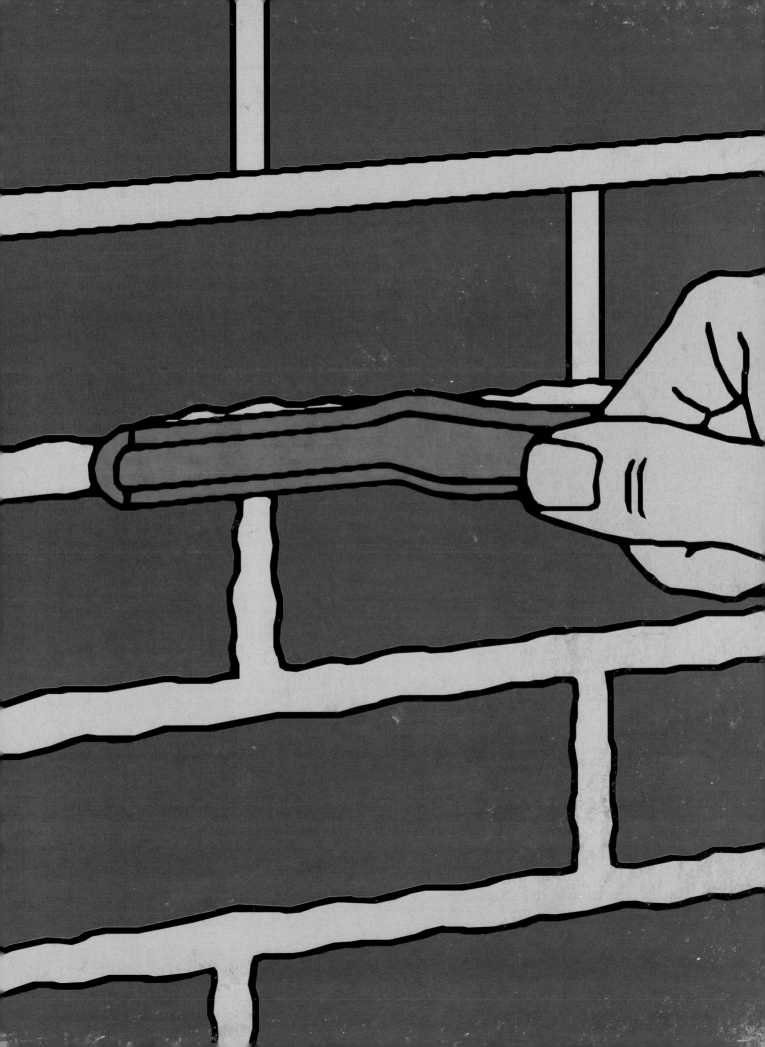

Mirrored Walls to Brighten a Room

Strategically hung mirrors have long been used to create a feeling of spaciousness in small rooms. Covering an entire wall with mirror tiles or panels can amplify that result, making such a room seem even lighter, larger, and more open.

Mirror tiles are made of thin glass that makes them lightweight but also tends to lessen their reflective quality. For a more distortion-free reflection, install mirror panels, which are made of thicker glass.

Mirror tiles attached to a wall with tape may be removed fairly easily; wear work gloves to protect your hands in case glass breaks. Installation with mastic, however, makes the mirrors a permanent part of the wall. Removing the glass panels is impossible without breaking them and seriously damaging the wall.

Installing Mirror Tiles: Available as 1-foot squares, mirror tiles are attached with a double-faced tape that is sold both in rolls and in precut squares. The tape works well on most smooth, very clean surfaces but will not adhere to vinyl wall coverings. Once you peel the protective cover from the tape, hold it only by the edges; skin oils can cause this tape to fail.

Mounting Mirror Panels: Heavier mirrors require supporting hardware, as well as the use of a mastic adhesive compounded specifically for mirrors. These mastics do not react with the silver on the mirror and are applied in thick pats that never harden. Because of this resilience, mastic can withstand sudden jolts—even a minor earthquake—that might otherwise jar the mirror loose.

When you buy mastic, ask the mirror dealer to recommend the one that is most suitable for the surface you intend to stick the mirror to. Some require covering the back of the mirror with a special bonding coat; read label directions carefully.

Planning the Layout: Although mirrors may be mounted wall to wall and floor to ceiling, walls frequently are not square. You can simplify your installation if you leave at least a narrow border of uncovered wall.

Tailoring mirrors to fit irregularities can be difficult. If you need smaller pieces of mirror to cover the desired area, the thin glass tiles are the only type that you can cut yourself *(opposite)*. Thicker mirrors require professional cutting.

Handling Mirrors

✔ A square foot of $\frac{1}{4}$-inch mirror panel may weigh more than 3 pounds. Work with a helper if the panels are larger than 12 square feet.

✔ If mirror panels do not come with protective wrapping, safeguard the silvered backing from scratches by placing sheets of paper between the panels. Drape a towel or blanket over the back of a larger mirror until it is ready to be mounted.

✔ When carrying a mirror more than 3 feet long, hold it vertically so it will not sag and break of its own weight.

✔ If you and a helper will be navigating stairs while carrying a heavy mirror, post the stronger person at the lower end.

✔ Always store mirrors on edge.

⚠ **CAUTION** *If a mirror starts to fall while you are carrying or mounting it, do not try to catch it. Get out of the way—quickly.*

 TOOLS

Carpenter's level
Chalk line
Glass cutter
Drop cloth
Hacksaw
Screwdriver

 **MATERIALS**

Mirror tiles or panels
Mirror tile adhesive tape
Black plastic tape ($\frac{1}{2}$")
Masking tape
J molding
Escutcheon nails ($\frac{3}{4}$")
Felt
Mirror mastic
Screws and plastic anchors
J clips
Adjustable top clips

 SAFETY TIPS

Work gloves not only protect your hands from the sharp edges of mirror tiles and panels but also shield the mirror backing from harmful salts and oils from human skin. Wear goggles when trimming thin mirror tiles.

MIRROR TILES: LOW-COST AND EASY TO INSTALL

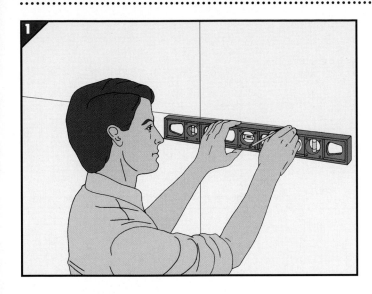

1. Laying out the tiles.

◆ Using a carpenter's level as a straightedge, mark a light pencil line around the perimeter of the area to be tiled.

◆ Using a chalk line as a plumb bob, snap a vertical guideline through the center of this area, between the upper and lower edges.

◆ Measuring down from the top of the vertical line, make a mark at the 1-foot measure closest to your eye level. Draw a level horizontal line through this mark to the ends of the tile area (left).

◆ Peel off the protective cover from one side of a square of mirror tile adhesive tape. Press the tape firmly to the back of a tile $\frac{3}{4}$ inch from a corner; repeat at the other corners. Attach tape to the other tiles.

2. Setting the tiles.

◆ Strip the outer paper from the tape on the first tile, place the tile in one corner formed by the guidelines, and press the corners of the mirror against the wall.

◆ Set tiles in rows, working outward from the center. Before sticking each tile to the wall, test it for fit against its neighbors, without uncovering its adhesive tape. Where the edges of an imperfect tile do not align exactly with the edges of adjoining tiles, place a strip of black plastic tape on the wall, butted against one of the adjacent tiles, to camouflage the misfit. Then stick the imperfect tile in place, leaving a slight gap along the edge that coincides with the tape.

◆ Install all of the full mirror tiles, leaving until last any area that requires cut tiles.

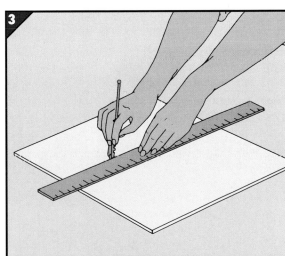

3. Cutting border tiles.

◆ Measure the gap to be filled by a partial tile, and mark a cutting line on the face of a tile with a felt-tip pen.

◆ Score along the cutting line with a glass cutter, using a straightedge as a guide. For best results, hold the cutter as shown above, start the scoring wheel $\frac{1}{16}$ inch in from one edge of the tile, and apply even pressure as you draw the wheel across the glass in one smooth motion.

◆ Wearing work gloves and goggles, align the scored line of the tile with the edge of a workbench. Break the tile by giving the protruding side a sharp downward snap.

◆ Affix adhesive tape in the corners of the cut tile and press it firmly against the wall.

MOUNTING BEVELED REFLECTING PANELS

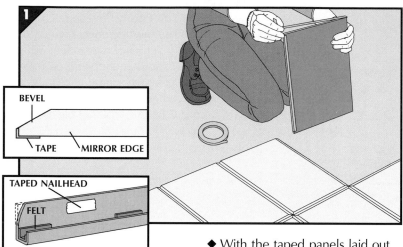

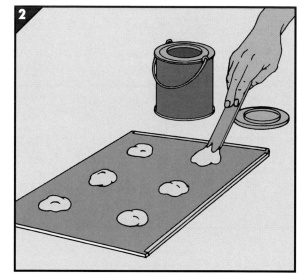

1. A dry run on the floor.
◆ On a carpet or drop cloth, lay out all of the panels as they will be placed on the wall.
◆ Pad each joint between panels with a single thickness of $\frac{1}{2}$-inch masking tape, cushioning the edges as shown above. Wearing work gloves, affix a strip of tape below the bevel and fold the excess onto the back of the mirror *(upper inset).*

◆ With the taped panels laid out on the floor, measure the bottom edge of the array. With a hacksaw, cut a section of metal J molding to this length, shaping the ends as shown in the lower inset.
◆ Draw a level guideline for the molding and then fasten it to the wall with $\frac{3}{4}$-inch escutcheon nails. Cover the nailheads with masking tape to keep them from scratching the mirror backing, and pad the bottom of the molding channel with squares of felt.

2. Applying mirror mastic.
With a wood paint paddle or a scrap of wood with a smooth end, daub pats of mastic onto the back of the mirror. For every square foot of mirror, apply four pats of mastic roughly $1\frac{1}{2}$ inches square and $\frac{7}{8}$ inch thick. Keep the mastic at least $2\frac{1}{2}$ inches from the edges of the mirror. If mastic begins to harden on the daubing stick, discard the stick and use a clean one.

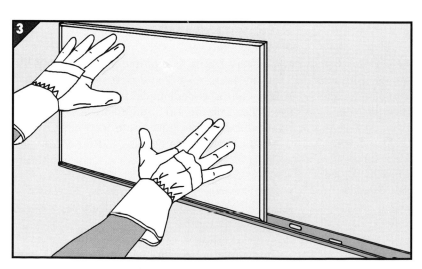

3. Installing the panels.
◆ Set the first mirror panel into the channel at one end of the J molding, then press the panel against the wall. Apply uniform pressure to the mirror surface until the mastic flattens and the back of the tile is approximately $\frac{1}{4}$ inch from the wall.
◆ Repeat this procedure to install a second panel against the edge of the first.
◆ Complete the bottom row of panels before you begin installing the rows above.
◆ After all the panels are on the wall, run a carpet- or foam-rubber-covered straightedge over the mirrors to correct their alignment and produce a flat plane.

SECURING MIRRORS WITH MASTIC AND J CLIPS

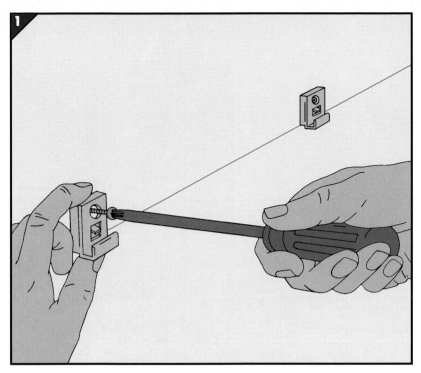

1. Bottom supports for big mirrors.

◆ Draw a level guideline along the wall to establish the position of the lower edge of the mirrors. Mark the locations of mirror-panel edges along this line.

◆ Measure from the bottom guideline to mark a line for the tops of the mirrors, checking it with a carpenter's level.

◆ With screws and plastic anchors, install two J clips for the bottom of each mirror, spacing one-third and two-thirds of the distance between panel-edge marks. If you use metal J clips, pad the clips *(page 44, Step 1)*.

◆ Cover all screwheads with masking tape.

2. Finishing the job.

◆ Above each clip on the bottom line, screw an adjustable clip *(photograph)* at the top line. Tape the screwheads.

◆ For every square foot of mirror, apply four pats of mastic as described on the facing page.

◆ With a helper holding the panel to prevent it from falling, tilt the top of the mirror away from the wall and lift the bottom into the J clips. Lift the tops of the adjustable clips and fit the mirror into them.

◆ Starting at the bottom, apply even pressure over the entire mirror surface, forcing it against the mastic until the panel is a uniform $\frac{1}{4}$ inch away from the wall.

◆ Install subsequent mirror panels edge to edge in the J clips. Press the panels evenly into the mastic so their reflecting surfaces form a perfectly flat plane *(page 44, Step 3)*.

Available in fine-grained sheet form and as square or rectangular tiles of coarser texture *(photograph, right)*, cork wall covering makes the perfect bulletin board or display area for a child's artwork. In addition, cork is easy to install and provides a measure of insulation against noise.

Once the cork is in place, removing it almost always damages not only the cork but also the wall. If you want a temporary surface, mount the cork on plywood or a wall divider *(pages 56-59)*.

Prior to Installation: To reduce expansion or shrinkage on the wall, unpack the cork and leave it for at least 72 hours in the room where it is to be mounted. Unroll sheet cork and flatten it with

weights as much as possible. Meanwhile, wash the wall and sand shiny surfaces such as glossy enamel to roughen them.

Mounting the Cork: Attach the cork to the wall with a latex-base adhesive of the type that is recommended for vinyl floor tile. However, if the cork might be subjected to dampness, as on the interior of an exterior masonry wall, coat the wall with a sealer to block moisture, and use a water-resistant, alcohol-base adhesive.

Spread the adhesive evenly with a notched trowel, and butt the sheets or tiles together without forcing them. Coat the completed wall, if you wish, with a cork sealer to protect it from dirt.

CORK TILE

CORK SHEET

 TOOLS

Framing square
Utility knife
Notched trowel ($\frac{1}{16}$" to $\frac{1}{8}$")
Rolling pin
Hammer
Nail set

 **MATERIALS**

Cork tiles or sheets
Chalk
Masking tape
Latex- or alcohol-base adhesive
Finishing nails
Cap molding

 SAFETY TIPS

When hammering nails, protect your eyes with goggles.

PUTTING UP CORK TILES

1. Cutting cork.

◆ Measure and mark the face of a cork tile for cutting. For a closer fit around irregular objects, first make a paper pattern, then outline the pattern on the cork with chalk to make a cutting line. To prevent breakage, apply masking tape over the cutting line and redraw the line on the tape.

◆ Place the cork on a work surface protected with heavy cardboard or hardboard. For straight lines, use a framing square as a guide to cut through the tile with a utility knife.

◆ To ensure smoothly fitting tiles, check the edges of all the tiles with a square, trimming them if necessary.

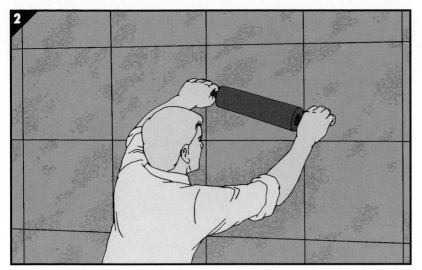

2. Pressing the tiles flat.
◆ Once you have cemented all the tiles to the wall, run a rolling pin over them. Apply firm, even pressure to remove all air bubbles and to force the back of each tile against the adhesive.
◆ If a tile breaks during installation, attach the pieces together on the wall; because of the cork's texture, the seam will not show.
◆ To adhere especially thick or rough-textured tiles to the wall, drive finishing nails partway into the center and all four corners of each tile until after the adhesive sets. Then either extract the nails with a hammer, placing a scrap of wood under the head to keep from damaging the cork surface, or drive the nails into the crevices of the cork with a nail set.

MOUNTING LARGE SHEETS OF CORK

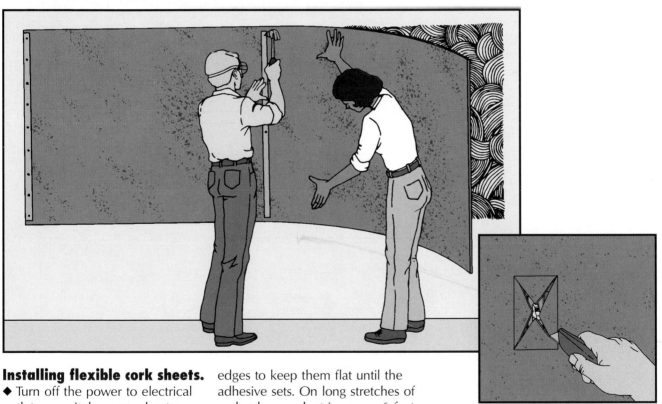

Installing flexible cork sheets.
◆ Turn off the power to electrical outlets or switches you plan to cover with cork and remove the faceplates.
◆ Outline the sheet on the wall and apply adhesive within the outline.
◆ With a helper, lay the cork sheet against the wall. Nail strips of scrap wood or plywood over any curling edges to keep them flat until the adhesive sets. On long stretches of cork, place such strips every 6 feet or so—or as close together as necessary to hold the cork against the wall. After the adhesive has set, remove the strips.
◆ To finish cork that does not cover an entire wall, frame it with cap molding *(page 79)*.

Trimming around outlets or switches.
◆ After the cork sheet is in place, find the outlet or switch openings by feel and, with the power turned off, cut a small X in the center of each. Carefully enlarge the X, using the corners of the electrical box as a guide, then trim the cork to match the edges.
◆ When the adhesive is dry, add a $\frac{1}{4}$-inch box extender to the electrical box to make the fixture flush with the cork surface *(page 27);* replace the faceplates.

The Practical Beauty of Brick Veneer

Brick veneer is an artful illusion. Composed of $\frac{1}{2}$-inch-thick slabs of real brick, this surfacing material offers all the warmth and charm of a solid brick wall at a fraction of the cost and weight.

Veneer Options: Two forms of brick veneer are available: individual bricks and preassembled brick panels. Loose bricks, glued to the wall with a special adhesive, come in a wide variety of colors, finishes, and textures. Panels contain about 36 bricks glued to a fiberboard backing that usually measures $16\frac{1}{2}$ by 48 inches. Fastened to the wall with nails, panels are easier to install than individual bricks, although obstacles pose more difficulties. Panels are also heavier and more expensive.

Preparation: Any wall used as a backing for individual bricks must be clean and free of wallpaper. If it is painted, score it with a pointed tool to roughen the surface for the adhesive. Baseboards must be removed, but you can leave window and door trim in place. The faceplates of electrical outlets and switches should be removed and their outlet boxes extended with special collars *(page 27)*.

Before installing either individual bricks or panels near a stove or fireplace, check with local authorities. Although the bricks themselves are fireproof, some fire codes require that they be backed with a fireproof material such as metal or cement-base panels.

Filling the Joints: The gaps between bricks—whether set individually or in panels—are filled with mortar. To mix the mortar from scratch, combine $2\frac{1}{2}$ parts sand, 1 part Portland cement, and enough water to thin the mixture to the consistency of applesauce. This is thinner than for conventional bricklaying because the mortar does not have to support the weight of the bricks. If you prefer to use a ready-mix mortar, add a tablespoon or 2 of liquid detergent to keep the mixture flowing smoothly.

Apply the mortar with a mortar bag *(page 51)* fitted with a nozzle equal in diameter to the space between bricks—usually $\frac{1}{2}$ inch. Before the mortar dries, smooth it with a tool called a jointer, which has a convex surface for pressing the mortar in against the edges of the bricks.

 TOOLS

Chalk line
Level (4')
Tile nippers
Putty knife
Mortar bag
Ruler
Hammer
Jointer ($\frac{1}{2}$")
Wire brush
Electronic stud
   finder
Nail set
Utility knife
Cold chisel
Notched trowel

 **MATERIALS**

Nails ($1\frac{1}{2}$" finishing,
  $1\frac{1}{2}$" roofing, $1\frac{1}{2}$"
  fluted-shank
  masonry)
Brick veneer
Veneer adhesive
Mortar
Fiberboard
  ($\frac{1}{2}$" thick)

 SAFETY TIPS

Wear goggles when cutting bricks, hammering, and chiseling.

Components of brick veneer.

You can refinish any wall with the brick types shown at right. Flat bricks, called stretchers, are used to cover most of the wall's surface. Half-sized stretchers, called headers, give the appearance of a brick seen end-on and serve to vary the pattern. Two-sided bricks wrap around wall edges, and three-sided bricks cover corners.

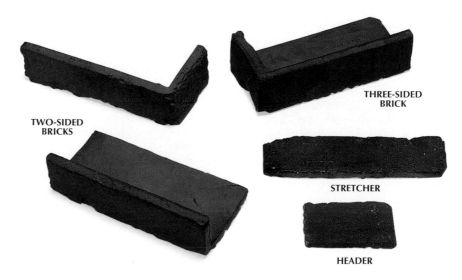

TWO-SIDED BRICKS

THREE-SIDED BRICK

STRETCHER

HEADER

MIMICKING THE LOOK OF REAL BRICK

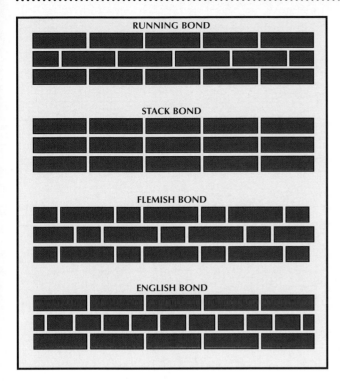

RUNNING BOND

STACK BOND

FLEMISH BOND

ENGLISH BOND

Choosing a pattern.
Veneer bricks can be arranged in any of the patterns used for structural brick walls *(left)*. Most common is the traditional running-bond pattern, in which stretcher bricks are set in staggered rows, or courses. Also popular is stack bond, although this pattern is difficult to align perfectly over large spaces. Flemish and English bond, combining stretchers and headers, are derived from Colonial houses in which header bricks joined the two layers of a double brick wall.

The number of bricks needed for each pattern varies but is generally six or seven bricks per square foot. To estimate how much you will need more precisely, lay out your pattern on the floor next to the wall for which it is intended, leaving about $\frac{1}{2}$ inch between the bricks for mortar.

SETTING INDIVIDUAL BRICKS

1. Measuring and marking courses.

Use this procedure for a wall without windows or other interruptions.

◆ At one end of the wall, make a vertical series of marks, spaced $2\frac{3}{4}$ inches apart, beginning at a point $2\frac{3}{4}$ inches above the floor. If the floor is not level, mark the wall at the higher end.

◆ Tap a nail into the first mark and tie a chalk line around it. Have a helper hold the line taut against the far end of the wall while you level it with a 4-foot level. When the chalk line is level, snap it; the mark left on the wall establishes the top of the first course, with room for a mortar joint below.

◆ Repeat for each mark along the wall.

If a window or door interrupts the wall, use the top of the window or doorframe, or the bottom of the window frame, as a starting point.

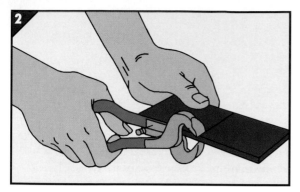

2. Cutting bricks to fit the pattern.

◆ Draw a pencil line across the back of the brick where the cut will be.

◆ Align the blades of the tile nippers with the pencil line and cut through the brick along the line.

◆ Smooth the cut by chipping away rough edges with the nippers.

3. Establishing the pattern.

◆ Start by installing a column of bricks up an inside or outside corner. On an inside corner, use header and stretcher bricks, alternating them as the pattern requires; wrap outside corners with two-sided bricks (inset).

◆ With a putty knife, apply adhesive to the back of each brick in $\frac{3}{4}$-inch daubs, about $\frac{1}{2}$ inch thick and 2 inches apart.

◆ Line the top of the brick against the chalked guideline and press it against the wall with a slight twisting motion to spread the adhesive, which will ooze out around the edges of the brick.

◆ Tap $1\frac{1}{2}$-inch finishing nails partway into the wall beneath two-sided bricks to hold them in place until the adhesive sets—from 48 to 72 hours; then remove the nails.

VENEERING IRREGULAR AREAS

Outlining an arch.

For this situation, use two-sided bricks with either the long or short ends facing out. Apply adhesive to each brick as in Step 3 above.

◆ Find the center of the arch and set a brick there, holding it in place with $1\frac{1}{2}$-inch finishing nails tapped partway in at an angle.

◆ Set a brick at each end of the arch and secure it with nails in the same fashion.

◆ Measure the distance between the center brick and each end to determine the spacing of the remaining bricks. Then, working on one half of the arch at a time, set the rest of the bricks (left).

Framing a raised hearth apron.

◆ Cap the corners of the hearth with three-sided corner bricks, then set two-sided bricks along the hearth edges. Space the bricks evenly across the edge, adjusting the distance between them as necessary to avoid cutting any bricks.

◆ Set bricks along the side edges in the same way.

◆ Then fill in the top of the apron with bricks in the pattern of your choice.

◆ Start veneering the apron sides by setting two-sided bricks down the vertical edges of the hearth apron, securing them with $1\frac{1}{2}$-inch finishing nails until the adhesive sets.

◆ Finally, fill in the sides of the apron with the pattern of your choice, securing these bricks with nails also.

FILLING JOINTS WITH MORTAR

1. Applying the mortar.

◆ After the adhesive has set, remove the supporting nails.

◆ Using a mortar bag equipped with a $\frac{1}{2}$-inch nozzle, fill the horizontal joints and then the vertical joints with enough mortar so that it bulges out slightly beyond the face of the brick *(right)*. To prevent dried mortar from clogging the nozzle, rinse out the mortar bag between fillings.

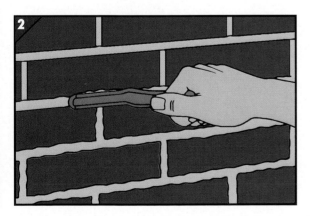

2. Tooling the joints.

◆ When the mortar is dry and crumbly to the touch—in about 20 minutes—smooth and flatten it with a $\frac{1}{2}$-inch jointer. Work the vertical joints first, pushing the mortar surface about $\frac{1}{8}$ inch be-low the face of the brick.

◆ When the mortar is completely dry, usually within 1 or 2 hours, rub the bricks and joints vigorously with a stiff-bristle or wire brush to clean them of mortar remnants.

MOUNTING BRICK VENEER PANELS

1. A base for corner bricks.

Each corner requires a pair of $\frac{1}{2}$-inch plywood or fiberboard framing strips. The exact width will be specified by the manufacturer, but in any case, one strip must be $\frac{1}{2}$ inch wider than the other to provide an even framing surface.

Nail the framing strips to each corner: For an outside corner, lap the wider strip over the narrower one; for an inside corner, set the wider one flush with the corner and lap the narrower one over it.

2. Nailing the panels.

◆ Using a stud finder, locate the wall's studs and mark them at approximately $16\frac{1}{2}$-inch intervals up the wall. If the floor is not level, snap a level chalk line across the wall $16\frac{1}{2}$ inches above the highest point of the floor.
◆ Butt a panel against the corner framing strip. Keeping its top edge against the chalked line, nail the panel to the wall stud nearest the corner (right). For wallboard or plaster walls, use $1\frac{1}{2}$-inch roofing nails driven through the panels, between bricks, into the studs. For cinder block walls, use $1\frac{1}{2}$-inch fluted-shank masonry nails. Use a nail set to get the nails flush with the backing.

3. Interlocking the panels.

◆ Have a helper pull the unattached end of the first panel away from the wall just enough to let you slide the adjoining panel into it until the two backing boards meet; then push both panels against the wall.
◆ Nail the second panel to the stud nearest the joining edge, then finish nailing the first panel to the wall; each panel should be anchored by at least 12 nails.
◆ Continue adding and interlocking the panels until you have installed the last full panel that fits across the wall.
◆ Then install panels in parallel rows above the one already in place.

To fill in gaps, measure the remaining spaces. Mark and score the back of a panel to fit each space, and cut through the board with a utility knife along the scored line. If you need to remove an entire brick that overlaps the cut, pry it off; to trim an overlapping brick flush with the cut, use a hammer and cold chisel.

4. The finishing touches.

Any remaining spaces must be filled with individual bricks; use the adhesive recommended by the manufacturer.

◆ Cover outside corners with two-sided bricks, supported with $1\frac{1}{2}$-inch finishing nails until the adhesive sets.

◆ Cover inside corners with flat bricks cut to size and temporarily supported by nails in the same manner.

◆ After the adhesive has set, remove the support nails and fill the mortar joints as shown in Steps 1 and 2 on page 51.

PLASTIC OR PLASTER MASONRY

Veneer bricks made of plastic or plaster can be almost as convincing as real brick veneer—and they are easier to install because you can cut them with a utility knife. The adhesive is applied to both the wall and the brick. Since it has a mortarlike texture and color, there is no need to fill joints with mortar.

Another veneering option is plaster stone *(right)*. Purchased in boxed sets, these facsimile stones have subtle variations in color and texture and are cut to fit together well.

Uncovering a Brick Wall

Many houses built before 1940 have interior walls made of brick covered by a layer of plaster. Stripping away the plaster to expose the brick often adds color, texture, and rustic charm to a room. Before beginning the job, however, remove a square foot of plaster in a lower corner to determine whether the brick is attractive enough to reward the work.

Preliminary Preparations: Although exposing brick involves few steps, the job takes at least 10 days and is dusty work. Remove from the room all furnishings and the contents of closets or cabinets. With masking tape, seal closet and cabinet doors, heat returns and registers, and all doors leading to other parts of the house. Archways and similar openings can be sealed with a dust curtain of plastic sheeting taped to ceiling and floor. Overlap the sheets about 8 inches.

Cover the floor with hardboard $\frac{1}{8}$ inch or more thick, followed by plastic sheeting at least 4 mils thick. Seal the plastic to the bottoms of the walls with duct tape.

Turn off the power to the wall and remove the cover plates, switches and receptacles, and outlet boxes. Also remove the wood trim along the wall except doorframes and window frames; leave these intact unless you plan to trim the jambs to match the exposed wall.

Sprucing Up the Wall: To match the color of the existing mortar when patching crumbling mortar joints, take a sample to a masonry supplier for help in custom-tinting a mortar mix. Muriatic acid for cleaning bricks is available at paint stores, as are a variety of masonry sealers in flat or glossy finishes.

> ⚠️ **CAUTION** *Old walls sometimes contain asbestos or lead. See page 13 for ways to deal with these hazards.*

 TOOLS

Bricklayer's hammer (18-oz.)
Wire brush with medium bristles
Cold chisel
Hammer
Pointing trowel
Stiff-bristled brush
Caulking gun
Paintbrush

 **MATERIALS**

Masking tape
Duct tape
Plastic sheeting (4-mil)
Hardboard ($\frac{1}{8}$")
Mortar
Flexible metal conduit
Muriatic acid
Masonry sealer
Latex or silicone caulk

 SAFETY TIPS

Goggles and a dual-cartridge respirator protect eyes, nose, and mouth from plaster dust and acid fumes. Work gloves keep hands safe from jagged plaster, while rubber gloves help prevent acid burns.

1. Breaking away plaster.

◆ Open windows in the work area for ventilation.
◆ Starting at the bottom of the wall, strike the plaster surface with a bricklayer's hammer at a 45-degree angle *(left)*. Pull cracked plaster away from the wall and strike succeeding hammer blows about 6 inches above the broken edge of the plaster.
◆ With the chisel end of the hammer, chip off stubborn clumps of plaster and pry plaster out of tight spots, as in corners and under doorframes and window frames.
◆ If the plaster has been laid over metal or wood lath, pry it loose and pull it off the wall with gloved hands.

2. Repointing the wall.

◆ Clean any remaining plaster off bricks with a wire brush.

◆ With a cold chisel and hammer, remove loose mortar around bricks and deepen the recesses for outlet boxes so that outlets and switches will be flush with the wall.

◆ If wiring has been exposed by the removal of the plaster, clear out mortar joints to a depth of 1 inch in a stepped path leading to the box. Slip a narrow, flexible metal conduit over cloth-covered cable. Without cutting the cable, fit it into the opened joints.

◆ Mix mortar and press it into gaps in the mortar joints with a pointing trowel, covering conduit where necessary. Fill in spaces around door and window frames.

◆ Allow new mortar to set for at least 48 hours.

3. Cleaning the wall.

◆ With windows wide open, pour 1 part muriatic acid into a plastic bucket containing 3 parts water.

◆ Wash the wall with the acid mixture and a stiff-bristled brush. Try to avoid spattering; if acid spills on the drop sheet, blot it with newspaper.

◆ Rinse the wall by scrubbing it twice with water.

◆ Let the wall dry for at least a week before proceeding.

CAUTION *Handle muriatic acid with care. If some splashes on your skin, flush it away with water, then apply a burn ointment. A stinging sensation in your nose or eyes is a signal to leave the room immediately. Flush the affected area thoroughly with water, and take a rest from the work until the stinging subsides.*

4. Rewiring and sealing the wall.

◆ Mortar all the surfaces inside an electrical-box recess.

◆ Slip the supply wire into the box and push it into the recess.

◆ Scrape away excess mortar, then press a board against the box to make it flush with the wall.

◆ Repeat for other outlets and switches.

◆ Let the mortar dry 48 hours.

◆ Brush a coat of masonry sealer over the entire wall.

◆ When the sealer is dry, reconnect switches and receptacles and replace the cover plates.

◆ Restore the baseboards and any other wood trim that was removed, refitting them at the corners if necessary.

◆ Caulk the joints between adjoining sections of brick and plaster wall, around doorframes and window frames, and between the baseboard and the brick wall.

Wall Panels to Divide and Decorate

Instead of building a solid wall to split up a room, you can often achieve the same result with a strategically placed divider that is lightweight and easy to build. The simplest dividers consist of a wood frame around a panel made of any material you like, from opaque plastic to latticework interlaced with a vine.

Building the Frame: The type of wood used for the frame is up to you, though the size of the lumber depends on the panel. Frames for light, thin panel materials like plastic can be built from 1-by-3s; for heavier panel materials you might use 2-by-3s or 2-by-4s.

In the dividers illustrated here, the panels are no more than $\frac{1}{4}$ inch thick and are sandwiched between a continuous strip of lattice attached to one side of the frame, and a continuous strip of quarter-round molding *(page 58)*. For panels thicker than $\frac{1}{4}$ inch, it is customary to use quarter-round molding on both sides of a thicker frame *(page 58)*, resulting in a stronger divider whose two sides are identical.

Floor-to-ceiling dividers are held in place with a channel of decorative molding nailed to the ceiling *(page 59)*, while H-style dividers are secured to the ceiling with angle irons *(page 59)*. Either frame should be $\frac{1}{4}$ inch shorter than the ceiling, so that its top edge will not catch against the ceiling when you are raising the divider into place.

 **TOOLS**

Hammer
Corner clamps
Carpenter's level
Straightedge

Circular saw, or
   handsaw and
   miter box
Tape measure
Scriber

 **MATERIALS**

Frame lumber
Carpenter's glue
Finishing nails (2")
Lattice strips
Panel material

Brads ($\frac{3}{4}$")
Quarter-round
   molding
Angle-iron braces
Hollow-wall anchors
Decorative molding
Wood screws

 SAFETY TIPS

Goggles protect your eyes when you are hammering, sawing, and working with power tools.

Ways to divide a room.
Wood-framed divider walls commonly take one of two basic forms that offer varying degrees of privacy. One is a single rectangle extending from floor to ceiling *(above, left);* the other, with air space above and below, is mounted in an H-shaped frame *(above, center).* Either can be used in multiples to stretch farther or to accommodate narrow panels *(above, right).*

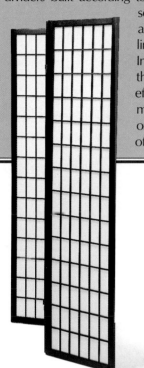

BUILDING A DIVIDER

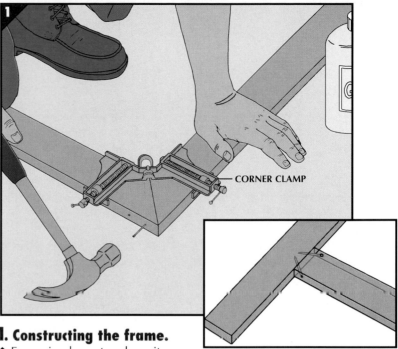

CORNER CLAMP

1. Constructing the frame.
◆ For a simple rectangle, miter four lengths of 1-by-3 lumber so that the inner edges are $\frac{1}{8}$ inch longer than the panel dimensions.
◆ Working corner by corner, apply glue to the mitered ends, then secure the frame pieces in a corner clamp.
◆ Drive 2-inch finishing nails into the joint from each direction *(above)*.

For an H-style frame, glue and toenail the top and bottom of the frame to the sides *(inset)*. Use a corner clamp to secure each joint while driving the first nail.

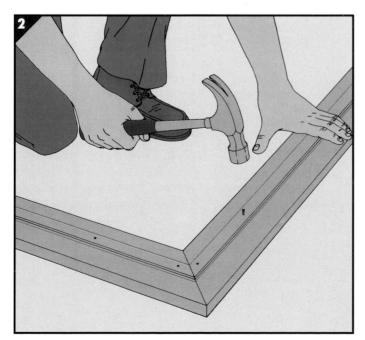

2. Tacking lattice to the frame.
If the difference between panel and frame thicknesses is an inch or more, secure the panel on both sides with quarter-round molding as described in Step 3. Otherwise, proceed as follows:
◆ Scribe a guideline around the back of the frame, $\frac{7}{8}$ inch from the inner edge.
◆ Miter cut four $1\frac{3}{4}$-inch lattice strips so their outer edges are the same length as the scribed lines.
◆ Apply glue to the back of the frame between the inner edge and the scribed line.
◆ Lay the lattice strips along the line and fasten them to the frame with $\frac{3}{4}$-inch brads at 6-inch intervals *(left)*.
◆ Turn the frame over and insert the panel, resting it on the lattice strips.

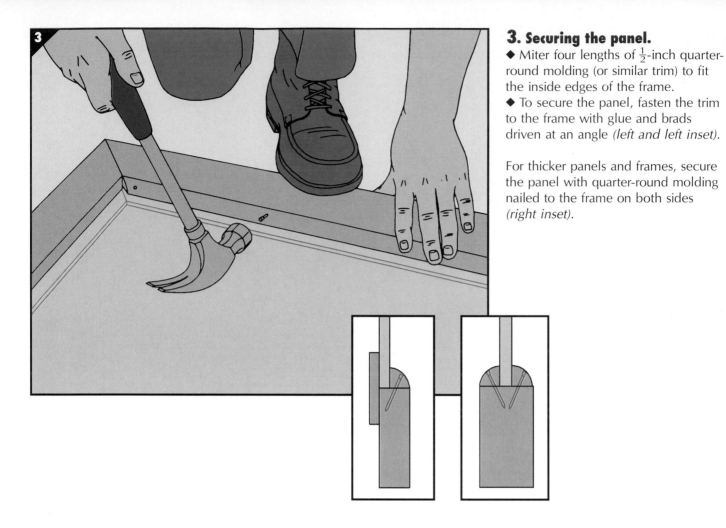

3. Securing the panel.

◆ Miter four lengths of $\frac{1}{2}$-inch quarter-round molding (or similar trim) to fit the inside edges of the frame.

◆ To secure the panel, fasten the trim to the frame with glue and brads driven at an angle *(left and left inset)*.

For thicker panels and frames, secure the panel with quarter-round molding nailed to the frame on both sides *(right inset)*.

LINKING FRAMES WITH LATTICE STRIPS

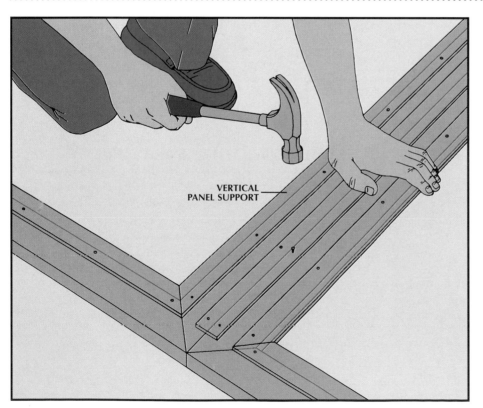

VERTICAL PANEL SUPPORT

Connecting divider panels.

◆ Cut a lattice strip to the same length as the vertical panel supports.

◆ Butt two panels together side by side, and fasten the strip evenly over the seam with glue and $\frac{3}{4}$-inch brads spaced 6 inches apart *(left)*.

◆ Carefully turn the frame over and fasten an identical strip of lattice to the other side.

ERECTING A DIVIDER

Bracing an H frame.
◆ Hold the divider in place and mark guidelines on the ceiling for two angle-iron braces.
◆ Then fasten angle irons to the ceiling, using expansion shields in plaster and hollow-wall anchors in wallboard.
◆ Raise the divider and attach the free leg of the angle iron to the frame *(inset)*.
◆ Check the panel with a level to make sure it is plumb, then toenail the bottom of the frame to the floor.

Securing a rectangular divider.
A three-sided, mitered channel anchors the divider to the ceiling and may serve the same purpose at the floor. For a ceiling channel, place the molding in the miter box upside down *(page 78)*. To fit the divider snugly against the wall, notch either the baseboard and its shoe molding or a corner of the divider frame.
◆ For the ceiling, cut two pieces of molding that are equal in length to the width of the divider plus the thickness of its frame; miter one end of each piece. Miter a third piece on both ends so that the inside edge equals the thickness of the divider frame.
◆ Glue and nail one of the long pieces of molding to the ceiling at the panel location.
◆ Raise the divider against the molding *(left)*, and nail through the molding into the divider frame.
◆ Place the second long piece of molding against the other side of the divider and fasten it to the ceiling.
◆ Fit the short piece of molding between the ends of the longer ones *(inset)*.

At the floor, adapt the foregoing procedure or anchor the frame with nails or screws driven at an angle into the floor.

Sturdier than a wall divider but quicker and easier to install than a wall framed with wood 2-by-4s, a metal-stud wall is a convenient way to partition a room. When covered with gypsum wallboard the finished wall is almost as rigid as the same material supported by wood studs; however, it is not as strong. Heavy items such as cabinets and book-shelves must be supported by additional wood framing.

The Components of the System: Metal framing, available from many building-supply distributors, consists of three-sided tracks, the sides of which angle slightly inward, and studs that fit into the tracks. The back—or spine—of each stud is stiffened with ribbing and has holes to accommodate electrical or plumbing lines.

Constructing the Wall: Assembly of metal framing begins with installing floor and ceiling tracks, which correspond to the sole and top plates of a wood-frame wall. In a doorway, the doorjambs are attached to wood studs screwed to metal ones.

When securing studs to the tracks, drive the screws with a screw gun or with a variable-speed drill fitted with a screwdriver bit. Metal studs cannot support the weight of wallboard panels installed horizontally. To finish the wall, arrange the panels vertically, as described on page 33, and fasten them with fine-threaded dry-wall screws.

TOOLS

Tin snips
Chalk line
Plumb bob

Caulking gun
Level
Electric drill with
  screwdriver bit or
  a screw gun

MATERIALS

Steel tracks and
  studs
Wallboard adhesive
2 x 4s

Plastic grommets
Fine-threaded dry-
  wall screws ($1\frac{1}{4}$")
Self-tapping pan-
  head sheet-metal
  screws ($\frac{1}{2}$" No. 8)

SAFETY TIPS

The edges of the metal framing are very sharp; wear work gloves when handling it. Protect your eyes with goggles when using the drill.

FRAMING A PARTITION WALL WITH STEEL

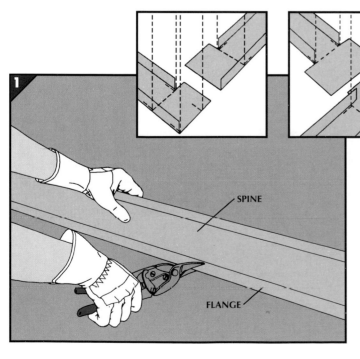

1. Preparing the tracks.

Trim tracks for the top and bottom plates with straight-cutting tin snips, severing the flanges first and then the spine.

To make a corner *(inset, above, left)*, transfer the in-side width of the spine to the flanges that will form the in-side of the corner. Cut the flanges, flatten them outward, then overlap the two sections

of track. When installing the studs *(Step 4, opposite)*, frame the corner with three studs *(dashed lines)* to support the wallboard.

Where one wall intersects another, cut and flatten the flanges as shown in the right-hand inset, then overlap the tracks. As with a corner, three studs are required. The two on the intersected track must be placed within 3 inches of the intersection.

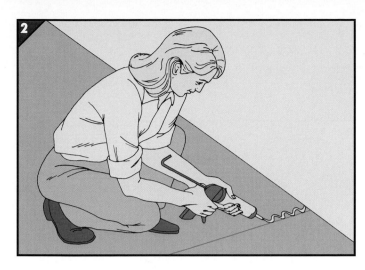

2. Laying the floor track.

◆ Snap a chalk line on the floor to mark the location of one edge of the track.

◆ With a plumb bob, mark two points on the ceiling directly above the ends of the floor line as a guide for the ceiling track.

◆ On the floor, apply a $\frac{3}{8}$-inch-wide bead of wallboard adhesive along the track side of the chalked line in a serpentine pattern.

◆ Press the track firmly into the adhesive, making sure the edge of the track is aligned with the chalked line.

◆ Secure the track to a wood floor with $1\frac{1}{4}$-inch dry-wall screws, 2 feet apart. Substitute fluted masonry nails if the floor is concrete.

3. Fastening the ceiling track.

Align the ceiling track with the two marks made in Step 2 and fasten it. If the track crosses ceiling joists as shown here, attach it to each one with a dry-wall screw.

If the track runs directly under a joist, fasten it with dry-wall screws, 16 inches apart. To install a track between joists, use hollow-wall anchors if the ceiling is finished. Otherwise, bridge the joists with 2-by-4 blocks nailed at 2-foot intervals. Screw the track to the blocks.

4. Erecting the studs.

◆ Cut studs $\frac{1}{4}$ inch shorter than the height of the new wall, trimming them at the top to keep the prepunched holes aligned.

◆ To preserve working space for attaching wallboard, place the end studs 2 inches from the existing walls. Set each stud edgewise into the floor and ceiling tracks, then turn it.

◆ Working from either end, install studs with their centers 16 inches apart, then plumb each one with a level.

◆ Fasten floor- and ceiling-track flanges to stud flanges with $\frac{1}{2}$-inch No. 8 self-tapping sheet-metal screws. To do so, clamp the track and stud flanges together with locking C-clamp pliers *(photograph)*. Unless you have access to only one side of the tracks, place a fastener on both sides.

MAKING WAY FOR A DOOR

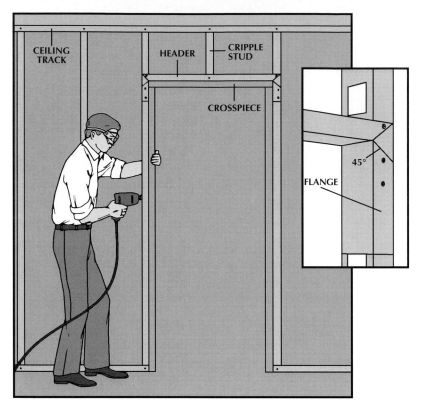

A frame within a frame.
◆ Determine the size of the rough opening required for the door.
◆ Install two metal studs—spines toward the door opening—3 inches farther apart than the width of the rough opening.
◆ Make a header from a piece of track 12 inches longer than the width of the opening. To do so, first mark the spine 6 inches from each end. Cut the flanges at a 45-degree angle, beginning about 5 inches from the ends, then bend down the ends to form right angles *(inset)*.
◆ Position the header $1\frac{1}{2}$ inches above the height of the rough opening and screw it to the studs.
◆ Attach an interior frame of 2-by-4s to the metal frame with $1\frac{1}{4}$-inch dry-wall screws driven through the studs and into the wood at 2-foot intervals. Be sure to rest the 2-by-4 crosspiece on the uprights.
◆ Cut a short cripple stud to fit between the header and the ceiling track and install it at the center of the door opening.

ROUTES FOR WIRING AND PLUMBING

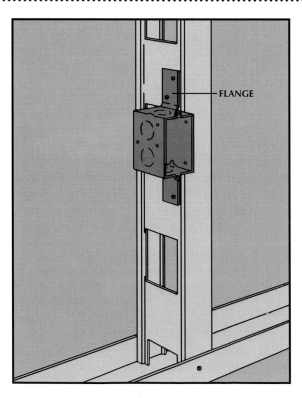

Installing an electrical box.
An electrical box that has flanges on one side is the easiest type to install in a new metal-stud wall. To mount the flanges on a stud, position the face of the box so that it will be flush with the wall surface; then secure the box with $\frac{1}{2}$-inch self-tapping sheet-metal screws.

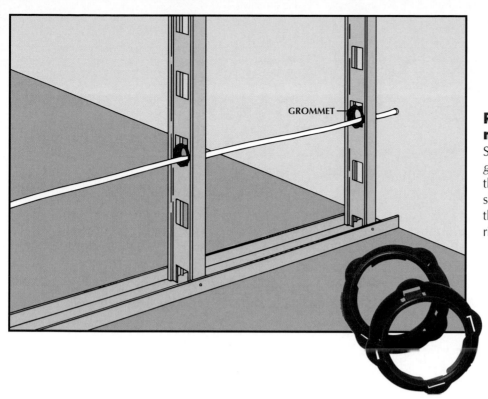

Running cable through metal studs.

Snap round plastic grommets *(photograph)* into the holes through which the cable will pass to protect it from sharp sheet-metal edges. Then thread the cable through the grommet-rimmed openings to the electrical box.

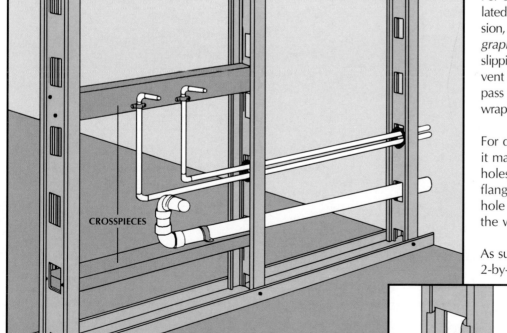

Securing pipes to metal studs.

For copper pipes, which must be insulated from steel studs to prevent corrosion, snap plastic grommets *(photograph, above)* into stud holes before slipping the pipes through them. To prevent the pipes from rattling where they pass through the studs, you can also wrap them with pipe insulation.

For drainpipes to fit through the studs, it may be necessary to enlarge the holes. With tin snips, cut toward the flanges at the top and bottom of each hole and bend the resulting tabs out of the way *(inset)*.

As support for the ends of pipes, cut 2-by-4 crosspieces to fit between studs. Install the crosspieces—either faceup or on edge, depending on the kind of support needed—and fasten them with $1\frac{1}{4}$-inch dry-wall screws driven through the studs and into the wood. Clamp the pipes to the crosspieces with pipe straps.

The Richness of Wood Paneling

3

The natural beauty of wood paneling evokes an age when trees were plentiful and skilled craftsmanship commonplace. Today's plywood paneling—surfaced in low-cost softwoods or choice hardwoods, with trim to match—can be hung in classic or imaginative patterns. For lovers of solid wood, hand-planed planks have given way to factory-milled boards that go up readily and last for generations.

Fitting diagonally mounted tongue-and-groove paneling →

Sheets of Wood Veneer for Walls

Nothing brings the warmth of wood to a room as quickly as paneling for the walls. Sheet paneling, whose installation is shown on the following pages, is far less costly than solid-wood boards *(page 80)* and easier to install.

Paneling comes in 4- by 8-foot sheets from $\frac{5}{32}$ inch to $\frac{1}{4}$ inch thick. It may be surfaced with real wood veneer or, at less expense and some loss of ambience, with simulated woodgrain printed on paper or vinyl *(chart below)*. Most styles have a vertical groove pattern, giving the appearance of individual boards.

Before You Start: To estimate how many panels you need for a room with 8-foot ceilings, measure the width of the walls in feet and divide by 4. Store the panels for 48 hours in the room where they will be used, stacked one atop another with small wood blocks between them. Remove any floor and ceiling molding in the room, as well as wall-mounted light fixtures and cover plates for outlets and switches.

Cutting and Securing the Sheets: Mark paneling on the back for trimming. To make a long, straight cut, use a circular saw; a saber saw is best for curved and short, straight cuts. Buy blades suitable for paneling: a plywood blade with 6 teeth per inch (TPI) for a circular saw, a blade with 10 TPI for a saber saw.

Paneling is best attached directly to existing wallboard or plaster if the wall is free of valleys deeper than $\frac{1}{4}$ inch. As a starting point, choose a corner of the room that allows paneling and wallboard joints to be staggered. Fasten panels to the wall first with panel adhesive—one 11-ounce tube for every three panels. Follow with paneling nails colored to match the finish and long enough to reach the studs in the wall.

To smooth out an uneven wall— or if working over a masonry wall— build a framework of furring strips *(pages 20-27)*. When paneling is attached to furring strips or to exposed studs in fire-prone areas such as halls, stairways, kitchens, and utility rooms, many fire codes require a layer of $\frac{1}{2}$-inch wallboard under the paneling.

 TOOLS

Electronic stud finder	Saber saw
Chalk line	Caulking gun
Carpenter's level (4')	Nail set
Tape measure	Block plane
Straight scrap wood	Plumb bob
Circular saw	Electric drill
	Hole saw

 MATERIALS

Scrap plywood	Wood blocks (8")	1 x 2 strips
C-clamps	Paint thinner	Wood glue
Panel adhesive	Parting bead ($\frac{1}{4}$")	Hinges
Shims	Chalk	Doorknob
Paneling nails ($1\frac{5}{8}$")		Catch

 SAFETY TIPS

Protect your eyes with goggles when hammering, drilling, or cutting with a power saw. Ventilate the room when applying paneling adhesive.

TYPES OF SHEET PANELING

Panel	Composition	Pros and Cons
Simulated pattern on hardboard	Heated and compressed wood fiber covered with paper- or wood-printed finish; $\frac{5}{32}$ or $\frac{3}{16}$ inch thick.	Great variety of styles; dulls saw blades quickly.
Simulated pattern on plywood	Plywood covered with a paper-, vinyl- or wood-printed finish; $\frac{5}{32}$ or $\frac{3}{16}$ inch thick.	Stronger and more flexible than hardboard; can be bent to fit curved walls; less costly than real wood veneer, but often thinner and less solid.
Wood veneer on plywood	Real wood veneer over a plywood backing; veneer can be hardwood or softwood; usually $\frac{1}{4}$ inch thick.	Texture and patina of real wood; best resistance to moisture, sound, and impact; each panel unique; more expensive than printed panels.

FITTING AND CUTTING PANELS

1. Establishing cutting lines.
◆ Locate studs *(page 8)* and mark each center with a chalk line. Extend the lines onto the ceiling and floor.
◆ At the corner of the room, position a 4-foot level horizontally against the wall, touching the ceiling. Measure any gap between the level and the ceiling where the gap is widest *(left)*.
◆ To mark a cutting line to match a sloping ceiling, turn the panel face-down. If the ceiling slants downward to the right as shown, mark the left edge of the panel with the width of the gap; otherwise mark the right edge. Draw a line from that point across the top of the panel to the opposite corner *(inset)*.
◆ Measure the distance from floor to ceiling at the corner of the room and 4 feet away from the corner.
◆ Subtract $\frac{1}{2}$ inch from both measurements and mark the distances on the sides of the panel, measuring from the top cutting line—or from the top edge of the panel if the ceiling is level.
◆ Draw a cutting line *(blue)* between the marks.

GAP

CUTTING LINE

HEIGHT OF CEILING AT LEFT SIDE

HEIGHT OF CEILING AT RIGHT SIDE

CUTTING LINE

$\frac{1}{2}$"

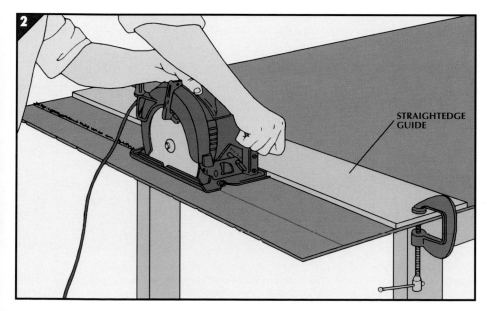

STRAIGHTEDGE GUIDE

2. Sawing the panels.
◆ Clamp a guide—the factory-cut edge of a sheet of plywood works well—to a scrap piece of wood, and make a short cut. Measure the distance from the guide to the cut.
◆ Use this measurement to position the guide parallel to the bottom cutting line. Clamp the guide securely and trim the panel *(left)*.
◆ Trim the top of the panel as marked to match the ceiling slope.

3. Applying panel adhesive.

◆ Spread adhesive in a continuous $\frac{1}{8}$-inch-wide serpentine bead on the wall surfaces that will underlie panel edges.

◆ Apply a similar bead of adhesive along the chalked lines marking the studs behind the panel *(left)*.

When fastening panels to studs or furring strips, apply adhesive where panel edges will fall as described above, but on intermediate studs or furring strips, apply the adhesive in 3-inch-long beads 6 inches apart.

4. Plumbing the first panel.

◆ Press the panel lightly against the adhesive, and wedge shims beneath it to lift it $\frac{1}{4}$ inch off the floor.

◆ Check that the panel is plumb with a 4-foot level held against the panel edge. Adjust the shims as needed to make the edge vertical.

◆ Secure the panel along the top edge with four $1\frac{5}{8}$-inch-long paneling nails. You may need longer nails if fastening through plaster and lath.

⚠ **CAUTION** *For a satisfactory paneling job, plumb this first panel precisely. If the grooves are not vertical, they will converge at corners, making it necessary to remove the paneling and start over with new panels.*

WOOD
BLOCK

5. Securing the panel.

◆ Press the panel against the wall to compress the adhesive. If the adhesive manufacturer requires it, pull out the bottom of the panel and insert an 8-inch wood block at each end, between the panel and the wall *(left)*. Let the adhesive dry according to the manufacturer's recommendation, then remove the blocks and push the panel against the wall again, tapping it with your fist to make a tight seal.

◆ With a rag dipped in paint thinner, wipe away any adhesive on the finished face of the panel.

◆ Nail the edges of the panel to the wall, spacing the nails 1 foot apart, then nail along the intermediate studs or furring strips at 2-foot intervals, placing the nails either in the grooves or $\frac{1}{8}$ inch from their edges.

◆ Set all paneling nails with a nail set.

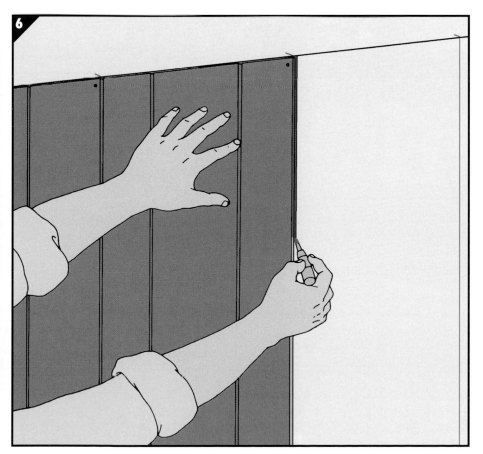

6. Setting adjoining panels.

◆ Stain the edge of the panel and the wall with a felt-tip pen the color of the grooves. Doing so keeps the joint between panels inconspicuous, even if the panels shrink.

◆ Tap paneling nails into the wall at the edge of the panel, top and bottom, to serve as spacers between panels.

◆ Install the next panel the same way as the first. To plumb it, butt it against the spacer nails, then remove them.

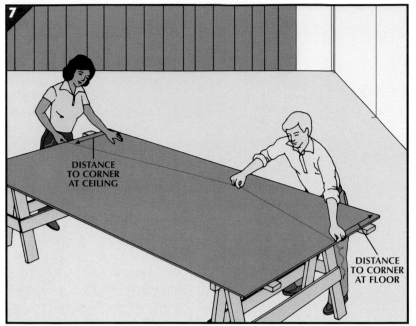

DISTANCE TO CORNER AT CEILING

DISTANCE TO CORNER AT FLOOR

7. Fitting a panel to a corner.

◆ Cut the corner panel to the proper height (*page 67, Steps 1-2*).
◆ Measure the distance from the corner of the room to the edge of the last panel installed, at both ceiling and floor. Mark these distances on the back of the corner panel so that the factory-cut edge will fall against the panel already in place.
◆ Snap a chalk line between the two marks (*left*) and cut along the line with a circular saw. Save the waste piece for possible use in another corner.
◆ Install the panel as you would a full-width panel, shaving the cut edge, if necessary, with a block plane for a perfect fit.
◆ Continue to panel around the corner by installing the first panel of the next wall as in Steps 1 through 5, using a level to plumb the panel. If this wall is less than the width of one panel, place the trimmed edge in the corner so you can use the factory-cut edge to plumb it.

PLOTTING CURVES FOR ROUNDED WINDOWS

VERTICAL COORDINATE

HORIZONTAL COORDINATE

VERTICAL COORDINATE

BASE

HORIZONTAL COORDINATE

VERTICAL COORDINATE

HORIZONTAL COORDINATE

1. Locating the center.

◆ Trim the panel (*page 67, Steps 1-2*).
◆ Remove any window moldings and mark the midpoint of the base of the semicircular window.
◆ Measure the distance from the ceiling to the midpoint of the base (*above*). Subtract $\frac{1}{4}$ inch for the clearance at the top of the panel.
◆ Measure from the center of the base to the edge of the last panel installed.
◆ Using these two distances as vertical and horizontal coordinates, plot the

center of the semicircle's base on the back of the panel so that the mark coincides with the center of the base when the panel is turned faceup.

If the semicircle is an arch framing the top of a door or window (*inset, top*), use the top of the rectangular section of windows as the base of the semicircle in the method described above.

For a circular window (*inset, bottom*), mark one side of the window where a

plumb bob from the ceiling just touches the frame, then mark the other side of the window in the same way. Measure the width of the window at these points and halve it to find the center of the window. From the center, find the vertical and horizontal coordinates as above and plot the center of the circle on the back of the trimmed panel.

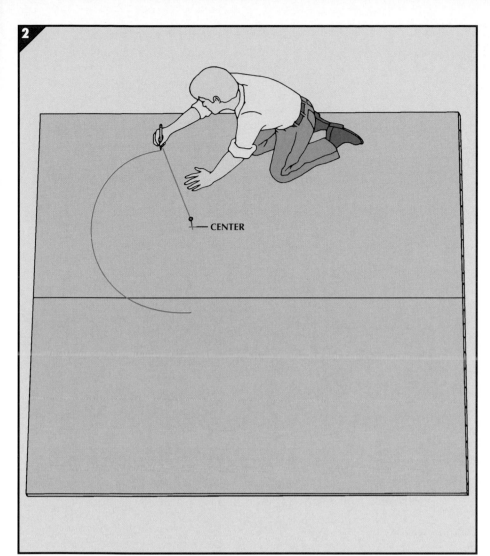

2. Drawing the curve.

◆ Tack a small nail or brad at the center point plotted on the back of the panel, taking care that the nail does not pierce the front of the panel.

◆ Tie one end of a string to the brad and attach a pencil to the other so the distance between the brad and the pencil point equals half the width of the base—plus $\frac{1}{4}$ inch for ease of fitting.

◆ Swing the pencil in an arc to draw the curve of the window frame. If the window falls at the joint between two panels, lay them facedown and side by side, reversed left to right from the order in which you will install them *(left)*.

◆ Draw any straight portions of the window outline, then cut out the opening and mount the panels.

◆ Before replacing window molding, cut a thin strip of $\frac{1}{4}$ inch parting bead and tack it to the edge of the window frame to serve as filler under the molding edge.

PANELING ODDLY SHAPED OPENINGS

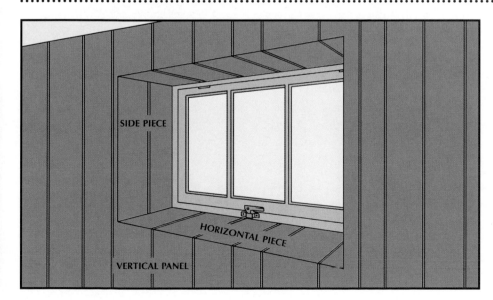

Making grooves turn a corner.

◆ When paneling a corner with horizontal surfaces, as found at a recessed window *(left)*, first cut paneling for the horizontal surfaces. If the opening falls within a single vertical panel, use the waste piece cut from it; vertical and horizontal grooves will align automatically. For an opening at a joint between panels, take care in trimming horizontal pieces so that grooves align. Install the horizontal pieces.

◆ Measure the sides of the window recess, cut waste pieces of paneling to fit, and install them.

◆ For a finished look, trim the opening with outside corner molding.

A pattern for an irregular shape.

◆ Tape paper over the opening, butting the sheet against the last panel installed and the ceiling. Outline the shape with a pencil *(left)*.

◆ Remove the paper, then cut out the shape with scissors and discard it.

◆ Turn the resulting pattern over and place it on the back of a trimmed panel. Align the side of the paper with the appropriate panel edge and the top of the paper $\frac{1}{4}$ inch below the panel's top edge to account for the space between the panel bottom and the floor.

◆ Mark the outline on the panel, then cut out the shape $\frac{1}{4}$ inch outside the line for ease of fitting.

◆ Install the panel.

ACCOMMODATING AN ELECTRICAL BOX

1. Chalking the edges.

To mark the location of an electrical box on paneling for a new wall, as in a false wall built over masonry *(pages 24-25)*, rub the front edge of the box, which typically protrudes beyond the studs, with a piece of chalk.

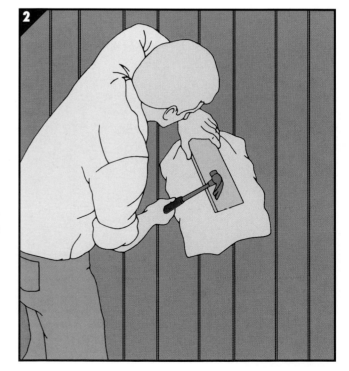

2. Transferring the shape.

Set the trimmed panel in its exact position over the box, and strike the face of the panel with a padded wood block to transfer the chalked outline onto the back of the panel. If the outline is not completely clear, use a spare electrical box as a pattern to fill in the missing sections with a pencil.

If paneling directly over an existing wall, a protruding switch or receptacle will prevent you from using the edges of the electrical box to mark the panel. Instead, plot the location of the box with coordinates, as described on page 30, and use a $\frac{1}{4}$-inch box extender *(page 27)* to make it flush with the paneling.

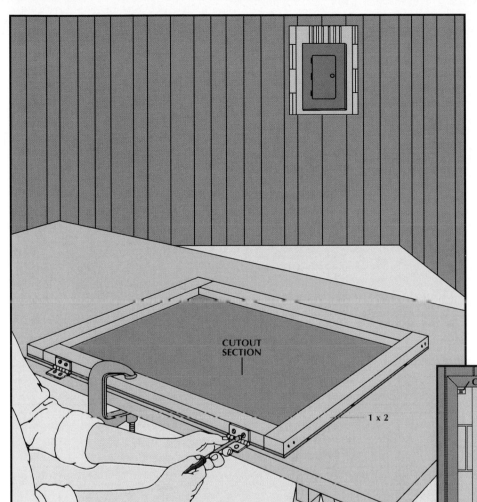

CUTOUT
SECTION

1 x 2

A door for a service panel.
◆ Measure the distances between the parts of the false wall *(page 25, inset)* that frame the service panel and use the system of coordinates shown on page 30 to mark the back of a panel for an opening of the same dimensions. Cut out the opening.

◆ Use the cutout section for a door, framing it with 1-by-2 strips glued to the back and screwed together at the corners.

◆ Screw hinges to one door edge *(left)*, set the door into the opening, then screw the hinges to the false-wall framing.

◆ Attach a knob to the front of the door, and a catch to the back and to a framing stud.

◆ For a more finished look, frame the opening with mitered molding *(inset)*.

CATCH

MOLDING

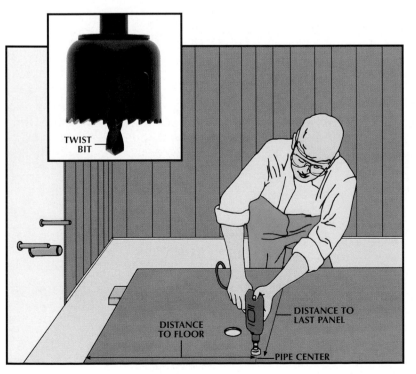

TWIST
BIT

DISTANCE TO
LAST PANEL

DISTANCE
TO FLOOR

PIPE CENTER

Perfect holes for protruding pipes.
◆ Establish the center of each pipe using the method for finding the center of a circular window *(page 70)*.

◆ Determine the vertical and horizontal coordinates, then transfer them to the back of a trimmed panel. Indent the points that represent the centers of the pipes.

◆ Cut a hole for each pipe, using a hole saw *(photograph)* $\frac{1}{2}$ inch larger than the pipe diameter. Drill only until the twist bit of the saw breaks through the face of the panel.

◆ Remove the saw, turn the panel over, and finish cutting the hole from the face side to avoid splintering it.

Not all walls are rectangular or 8 feet tall, and some have irregular edges or other unusual features. For such situations, you will need to cut panels in special ways.

Stairs: On stairway walls, you must trim the panels to match the diagonal of the stringers—the boards that frame the steps. In many cases only one end of the panel is involved—the bottom edge above the stringer or the top edge below the staircase. But if the stairwell has a slanted ceiling, both the top and the bottom of the panel must be angled. On a finished wall, you must transfer the stringer angle to the panel *(below and opposite, top)*.

High Walls: When a wall is taller than your panels you have several options. You can special-order extra-

tall panels, or you can leave a gap along the bottom of the paneling and cover the gap with baseboard, but this extends the paneling only a few inches.

A third option is to put up panels one atop the other until they reach the ceiling. They can be stacked vertically, horizontally, or in a herringbone pattern *(page 77)*. This zigzag design will extend the height 6 inches, but the assembled pieces will be 34 inches wide instead of 48.

A herringbone wall looks best when all the panels are the same width. Divide the wall into equal sections of 34 inches or less and trim panel pieces to that width. Since the edges no longer fall at studs, panels or furring strips *(pages 21-24)* must be attached to walls using the technique in Step 2 on page 93.

 TOOLS

Tape measure
Framing square
Chalk line
Plumb line

Scriber or compass
Coping saw
Long, straight board

 **MATERIALS**

Wood paneling
Cap molding
Flat molding

 SAFETY TIPS

Goggles and earplugs will guard your eyes and ears while you are running a power saw. Wear goggles when hammering nails as well.

SHAPING PANELS TO A STAIRCASE

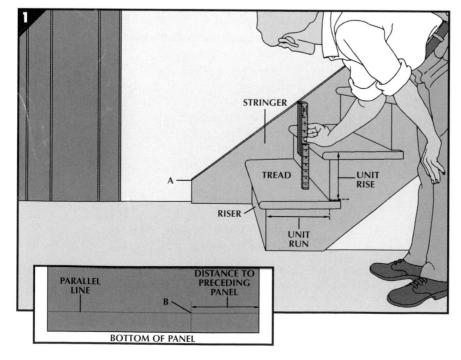

STRINGER

TREAD

UNIT RISE

RISER

UNIT RUN

A

PARALLEL LINE

DISTANCE TO PRECEDING PANEL

B

BOTTOM OF PANEL

1. Finding the stringer angle.
◆ Measure the unit rise—the distance from the top of one tread to the top of the next.
◆ Find the unit run—the distance between the front of one riser to the front of the next.
◆ From the point where the stringer begins to slope upward (A), measure both to the floor and to the edge of the panel most recently installed.
◆ Transfer these dimensions to the back of the panel to be installed at the bottom of the stairway *(inset)*. The point where they intersect (B) corresponds to A.
◆ Draw a line through B, parallel to the bottom of the panel across its entire width.

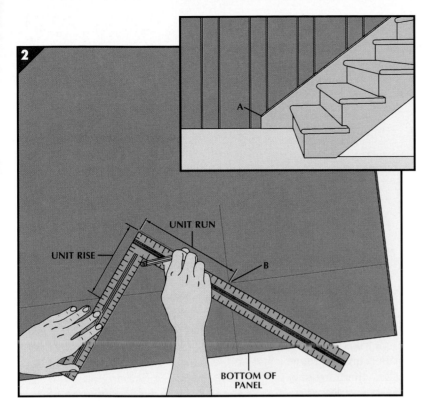

2. Marking the angle.

◆ Place a framing square on the back of the panel as shown at left, with one leg passing through B.
◆ Adjust the square so that the unit-run measurement, read on the outer scale of the square, rests at B while the unit-rise measurement intersects the line drawn parallel to the bottom of the panel.
◆ Draw the unit run on the back of the panel, then extend this line—which corresponds to the top edge of the stringer—across the panel.
◆ Place the remaining panels to be installed facedown alongside the first one, top edge and bottom edges even.
◆ Use a chalk line to continue the slanted line across the panels until it crosses the top edge of a panel.
◆ Cut the panels along this line *(page 67)* and along the line that runs from B to the bottom of the first panel.
◆ Install the panels *(inset)* as shown on page 68. Where the top edges do not abut the ceiling, conceal the gaps with cap molding *(page 79, top)*.

CONTOURING AROUND AN IRREGULAR SHAPE

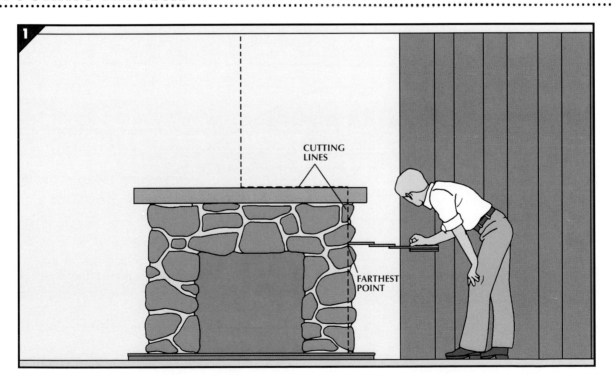

1. Measuring for a fireplace cutout.

◆ Install paneling, as shown on pages 66-69, to within 4 feet of the irregular edge of the fireplace.
◆ For a vertical cutting line at the corner of the panel that will meet the fireplace, measure the distance from the panel last installed to the farthest point on the fireplace edge *(above)* and mark the back of the panel accordingly.

◆ For a horizontal cutting line, measure from the ceiling to the mantel top, subtracting $\frac{1}{4}$ inch for clearance at the ceiling line and taking into consideration any ceiling irregularities *(page 67, top, inset)*. Mark this distance on the panel, measuring from the top.
◆ Cut out the waste rectangle defined by the vertical and horizontal lines.

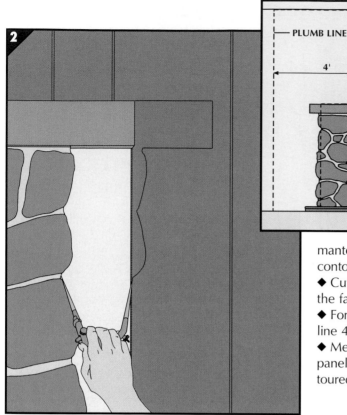

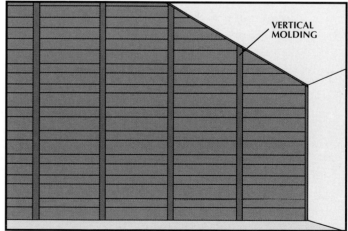

PLUMB LINE

4'

2. Scribing the panel.

◆ Set the newly cut panel against the end of the mantel, keeping the grooves plumb.

◆ Open a scriber or compass to span the distance between the panel edge and the point on the fireplace farthest from it, identified in Step 1. For best results, use a scriber or compass having a clamp to hold the setting.

◆ Starting at the top corner of the mantel and keeping the legs of the compass horizontal, transfer the contour of the fireplace edge onto the panel *(left)*.

◆ Cut out the fireplace shape with a coping saw to avoid splintering the face of the panel, then fit the panel to the fireplace.

◆ For the other side of the fireplace, have a helper hold a plumb line 4 feet from the edge of the panel you just installed *(inset)*.

◆ Measure from the plumb line to the most distant point on the un-paneled edge of the fireplace, then mark and cut a second contoured panel as you did the first.

STACKING PANELS FOR EXTRA HEIGHT

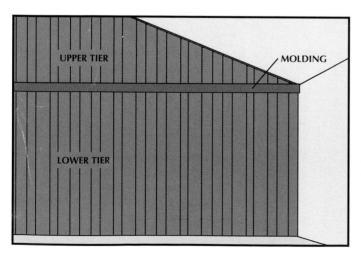

UPPER TIER

MOLDING

LOWER TIER

VERTICAL MOLDING

Vertical panels.

To cover a wall up to a high ceiling, install panels vertically in two tiers—the first extending from the floor up 8 feet, the second butted against the first and continuing to the ceiling. Make sure the grooves of both tiers are aligned. Cover the horizontal joint between tiers with flat molding.

Horizontal panels.

A second way to cover a wall up to a high ceiling is to stack panels horizontally, aligning the grooves of abutting panels. Cover the vertical joints with flat molding. As shown here, additional molding strips reestablish a vertical orientation for the paneling by interrupting the strong horizontal pattern of grooves.

A HERRINGBONE PATTERN FROM VERTICAL GROOVES

1. Marking the panels.

◆ On the back of a panel, mark the midpoint of both sides.

◆ Draw a cutting line from each midpoint to the diagonally opposite corner using a straight board.

◆ From the midpoint of each diagonal line, draw a second cutting line to the nearest corner.

◆ Label the panel edges SIDE A and SIDE B as shown at right.

◆ Similarly mark a second panel, but reverse the direction of the diagonals and label the sides C and D.

◆ Cut both panels facedown with a circular saw guided by a straight board, and discard the top and bottom triangles as waste (inset).

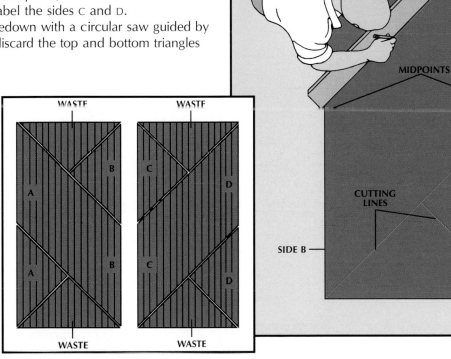

2. Fitting the pieces.

◆ Lay the pieces flat on the floor, butting together two A sides to form the top of a new rectangle and two B sides to form the bottom.

◆ Repeat this procedure for the C and D sides to form the adjoining rectangle, with the grooves running in the opposite direction.

◆ Using the measurements you obtained from dividing the wall into equal sections, mark the assembled panels to that width and cut them at the marks.

◆ Attach the first two sections of paneling to the wall, then cut and install subsequent sections, aligning the grooves to form a continuous herringbone pattern.

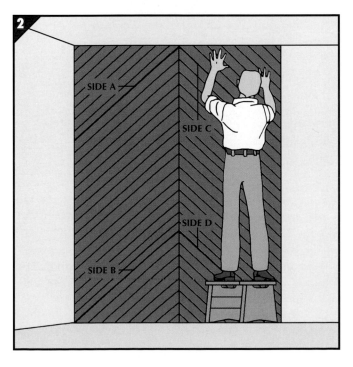

When panels are installed professionally, every exposed edge except the inconspicuous vertical joint between panels is covered by a molding. Typically the moldings hide gaps or unfinished edges at the floor *(right)*, ceiling, corners, and tops of paneling that extends only partway up a wall *(opposite)*. As a bonus, moldings speed installation by making precise measuring, scribing, and cutting less essential.

Fine Points of Nailing: To fasten panel moldings, use the same colored paneling nails that are supplied by the manufacturer for fastening the panels. Space the nails at 16-inch intervals, starting at a stud or furring strip, and drive the nailheads below the surface with a nail set.

TOOLS

Coping saw
Backsaw
Miter box
Sanding block
Hammer
Nail set
T bevel

SAFETY TIPS

Goggles protect your eyes when you are driving nails into molding or paneling.

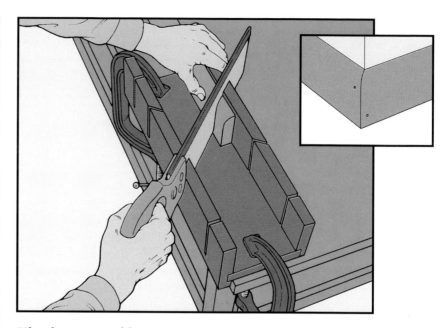

Mitering an outside corner.
◆ Miter both pieces of molding outward at a 45-degree angle, making the front face of the molding longer than the back face.
◆ Test-fit the pieces. If the joint has a gap at the front, sand the back edges of the boards to make them meet satisfactorily. For a gap at the back of the joint, sand the front edges.
◆ Drive a finishing nail through each side of the corner to pull the joint tight *(inset)*.

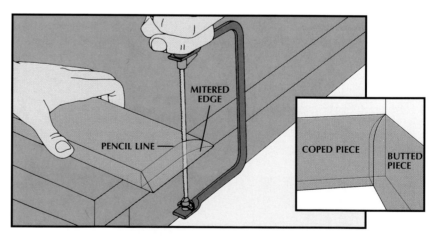

Dealing with an inside corner.
A coped joint permits molding to expand and contract with changes in temperature and humidity without opening a gap where molding pieces meet.
◆ Make a square cut at the end of one piece of molding for a corner. Butt it against the corner and nail it in place.
◆ Miter the end of the other piece at a 45-degree angle, cutting it so that the back face is longer than the front.
◆ With a pencil, highlight the curved edge of the miter cut, then cut along the curve with a coping saw. For a snug fit, angle the blade to back-cut the piece a few degrees, making the front face slightly longer than the back.
◆ Push the shaped end against the face of the butted molding already on the wall *(inset)* and nail in place.

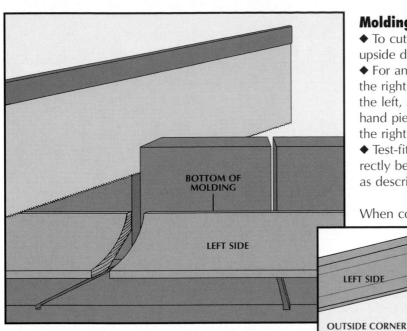

Molding at the ceiling.

◆ To cut cove molding for ceiling corners, place the pieces upside down in the rear corner of a miter box.

◆ For an outside corner, position the left-hand molding to the right of the 45-degree cutting slot that angles the saw to the left, and make the cut as shown here. Place the right-hand piece to the left of the slot that angles the blade to the right.

◆ Test-fit the joint at the corner with the pieces placed correctly between wall and ceiling *(inset),* and adjust for gaps as described *(opposite).*

When coping an inside corner *(opposite),* angle the saw to the right when mitering a left-hand piece, to the left for a right-hand piece. Slant the coping saw for a 30-degree back cut.

BOTTOM OF MOLDING

LEFT SIDE

LEFT SIDE

OUTSIDE CORNER

INSIDE CORNER MOLDING

OUTSIDE CORNER MOLDING

Hiding corner joints.

◆ Cut corner molding to fit snugly between baseboard and ceiling molding. At an inside corner, use concave molding; outside corners require convex molding.

◆ Fasten the molding to the wall, nailing concave molding in the center *(inset)* and convex molding through alternate sides.

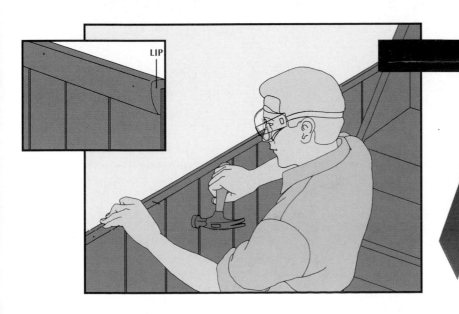

LIP

Cap molding for panel edges.

Cover the top edges of panels that end partway up the wall with cap molding.

◆ Fit the molding's lip over the top edges of the panels, then nail it through the paneling and into the wall.

◆ Set a T bevel *(photograph)* to the angle where the cap molding meets a stairway, then transfer that angle to the molding and cut it.

◆ At an outside corner, miter the molding; at an inside corner, use the coping technique shown on page 101.

Solid-wood paneling can bring formal elegance or rustic warmth to a room, depending on the choice of wood (such as rich mahogany or casual pine), the grade—which indicates the degree of knottiness—surface texture (smooth or rough-sawn), and pattern (*below*).

Buying Panels: Calculating amounts depends on installation pattern, average width of boards, and in some cases whether they are hard- or softwood. Ask a lumber dealer for help.

Preparing for Installation: So the boards will adjust to the temperature and humidity of the room to be paneled, store them there for at least 2 days before you start installation. To reduce warping, stack the boards in layers separated by scrap wood strips. If staining later, stain tongues or overlapped edges before installation.

While the boards acclimate, prepare the wall with furring strips unless you are using a diagonal pattern (*page 86*). Horizontal strips (*page 82*) are adequate for vertical (and diagonal) installation; furring for a herringbone pattern is shown on page 90. Attach the furring strips using the techniques on pages 20 to 24, but leave a $\frac{3}{4}$-inch space all around the opening for a door or window.

Adding Trim: After installing all the wall panels, add jamb extensions (*page 27, Step 2*) for the door and window trim. Cut trim strips from the same wood as the paneling and miter the corners to form a simple frame. Elsewhere, molding is optional, but base, ceiling, and corner molding can accent the room and cover inconsistencies in measuring and cutting (*pages 78-79*).

 TOOLS

Tape measure
Carpenter's level
Torpedo level
Scriber
Block plane
Hammer

Nail set
Electric drill
Saber saw
Circular saw
Chalk line
Steel square
Combination square
Paintbrush

 MATERIALS

Solid-wood
  paneling
1 x 4 furring strips
1 x 2 battens
Common nails
  ($3\frac{1}{4}$")

Finishing nails (2")
Wood glue
Brads
Wood filler
Wood stain
Polyurethane finish
Construction
  adhesive

SAFETY TIPS

Goggles protect your eyes while you are hammering and sawing. When staining and finishing, wear vinyl or rubber gloves. A dual-cartridge respirator filters toxic fumes produced by some stains and finishes.

CHOOSING PATTERNS AND EDGES

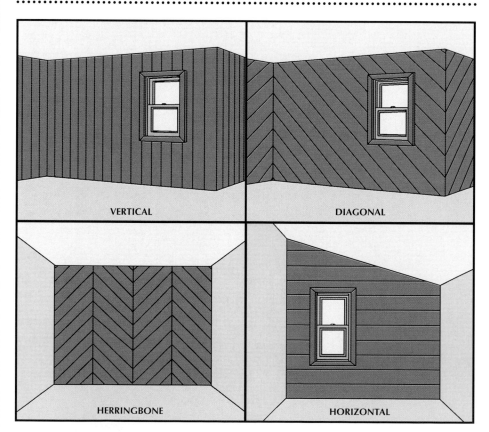

VERTICAL

DIAGONAL

HERRINGBONE

HORIZONTAL

Patterns for every purpose.

Installing boards vertically is most versatile. Smooth, polished woods and elaborate trim give a traditional, formal look. Choose rougher woods and a minimum of trim for a contemporary look.

Diagonal and herringbone patterns are best in a modern setting and on walls with few doors or windows. Diagonal boards on adjoining walls can be placed for a chevron effect as shown here or to continue the same slope.

Horizontal paneling reduces apparent ceiling height. Stagger the joints in each course to avoid unsightly vertical seams.

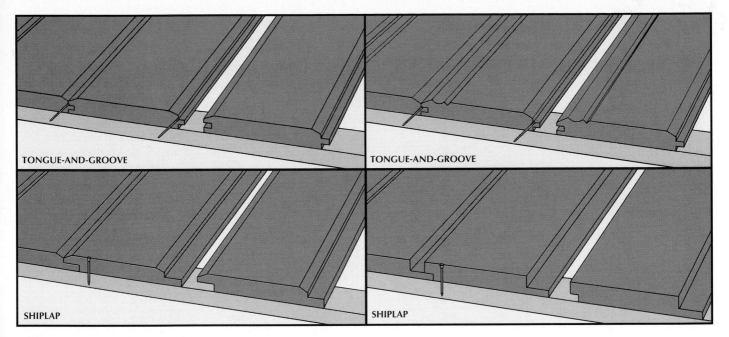

TONGUE-AND-GROOVE

TONGUE-AND-GROOVE

SHIPLAP

SHIPLAP

Milled edges for tight joints.

Solid-wood paneling has characteristic overlapping edges to prevent gaps between boards as they contract with atmospheric changes. A single row of nails per board keeps forces of expansion from loosening the boards.

Tongue-and-groove boards are easy to install in any pattern. Edges can be milled to create V-shaped seams between boards *(top left)* or more elaborate joints *(top right)*. The boards are blind-nailed to furring strips through the base of the tongue; nails are hidden by the next board.

Shiplap boards, which simply overlap each other, are best suited to vertical or horizontal patterns. The boards typically come beveled to form V-shaped seams *(bottom left)* or come with square edges *(bottom right)*, which produce a gapped joint. Shiplap boards are nailed through the face.

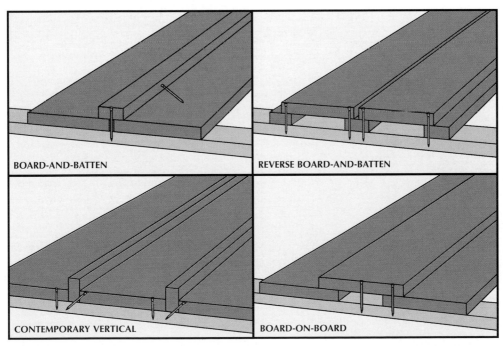

BOARD-AND-BATTEN

REVERSE BOARD-AND-BATTEN

CONTEMPORARY VERTICAL

BOARD-ON-BOARD

Edges for a modern look.

Straight-edged boards and battens installed vertically or horizontally produce a casual, contemporary effect.

Board-and-batten and reverse board-and-batten patterns are made of wide boards set about $\frac{1}{2}$ inch apart with a narrower batten—generally a 1-by-2—nailed either over or under the gap. The contemporary-vertical pattern uses battens set on edge between the wider boards.

Board-on-board paneling is similar to board-and-batten, except all the boards are the same width and the gap between boards in the first layer is about half the width of the boards.

With any of these patterns, when face-nailing is necessary, forestall splitting by blunting the nails and placing them as far as possible from board edges.

CLASSIC VERTICAL PANELING

1. Planning the layout.

To avoid a narrow strip as the last board on a wall, proceed as follows:

◆ After attaching furring strips to the walls, measure the length of the wall between corners formed by the strips *(left)*; if the wall has an outside corner, add $\frac{3}{4}$ inch. Divide this measurement by the width of a board measured from the top of the groove on one edge to the base of the tongue on the other.

◆ If the result ends in a fraction smaller than $\frac{1}{2}$, begin paneling the wall with a board cut in half lengthwise.

TRICKS OF THE TRADE

Easy Scriber

A carpenter's pencil can act as a scriber in an uneven corner. Stand a panel board in the corner, against the adjoining furring strip. Use a level to move the board into a plumb position, then press one side of the carpenter's pencil against the furring strip, and run the lead carefully down the board to mark it for trimming *(below)*.

2. Starting off plumb.

◆ Measure the starting corner from floor to ceiling and use a circular saw to cut a board to that length.

◆ Stand the board in the corner as shown at left, with the grooved edge abutting the furring strip on the adjoining wall, and check for plumb with a carpenter's level.

◆ If the grooved edge does not fit uniformly against the strip—and if the gap will not be covered by the edge of a panel board or corner mold-ing—scribe the board to match the corner. Use the technique on page 76, Step 2, or a carpenter's pencil *(above)*. Trim the edge to the mark with a block plane.

If you install the first board at an outside corner, where the adjoining wall will not be paneled, trim $\frac{1}{2}$ inch from the grooved edge of the board and place that cut edge plumb and flush with the corner. Plane as necessary for a precise fit.

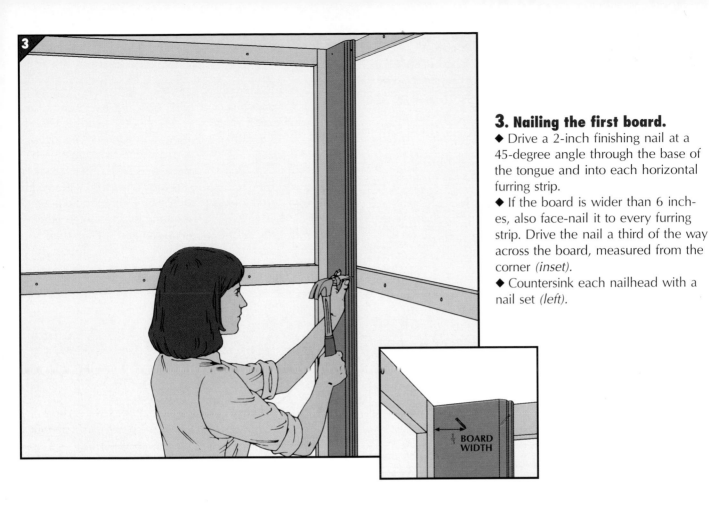

3. Nailing the first board.

◆ Drive a 2-inch finishing nail at a 45-degree angle through the base of the tongue and into each horizontal furring strip.

◆ If the board is wider than 6 inches, also face-nail it to every furring strip. Drive the nail a third of the way across the board, measured from the corner *(inset)*.

◆ Countersink each nailhead with a nail set *(left)*.

⅓ BOARD WIDTH

4. Fitting individual boards.

◆ To adjust each paneling board to slight variations in ceiling height, cut a piece of scrap lumber 3 inches shorter than the average ceiling height to use as a measuring template.

◆ Place the template where the next board will go, rest it on the floor, and measure from the top of the template to the ceiling *(above, left)*.

◆ Lay the template on the board to be cut, bottom ends flush, and transfer this measurement to it *(above, right)*.

◆ Cut the board at this point and slide it into place on the wall, grooved edge over the tongue of the previous board.

5. Locking the joints.

◆ To tighten the joint between two boards, cut a scrap of paneling about a foot long and use it as a hammering block.

◆ Slip its groove over the tongue of the outer board and gently tap the edge of the block until the joint is tight *(right)*. Then move the block along the board, closing the entire joint.

◆ Check the board for plumb, readjusting the joint at top or bottom if necessary, and nail the board in place.

6. Paneling around an opening.

◆ When you reach an opening such as a window, tap a full-length board in place.

◆ Mark the horizontal furring strips at the top and bottom of the opening where the tip of the board's tongue crosses them.

◆ Reach behind the board and mark the back along the inside edge of the same strips *(left)*. Then ease the board off the wall.

◆ Measure from the marks on the top and bottom furring strips to the inside edge of the vertical furring strip.

◆ With this measurement, mark a notch on the back of the board to fit around the window *(inset)*. Next, drill a $\frac{1}{4}$-inch hole in each corner of the notch to help a saber saw make the turn, and cut out the notch and install the board.

◆ Measure and cut paneling to fit above and below the opening.

◆ Finally, cut a board to fit the other side of the opening as above.

TOP STRIP

INSIDE EDGE

VERTICAL STRIP

BOTTOM STRIP

MAKING NEAT, TIGHT CORNERS

Mitering for an outside corner.

◆ Tap the corner board onto the tongue of the preceding board and mark the corner line on the back of the corner board *(right)*.

◆ Remove the board and clamp it facedown on two sawhorses with a straight 1-by-2 on top to guide a saw.

◆ Set the blade of a circular saw at a 45-degree angle and, with the blade pointing toward the tongue, cut along the corner line.

◆ Lock the board in place, with the beveled edge extending beyond the corner *(inset),* and nail it to the furring strips.

◆ To miter the adjoining corner board, draw a guideline on the back of the board at the width determined by the procedure described in Step 1 on page 82, measured from the base of the tongue.

◆ Clamp the board facedown and cut along the line, with the saw blade angled toward the board's grooved edge.

◆ Before setting the board in place, spread wood glue on both beveled edges. Pin the boards together with brads, then

set the brads. Let the glue dry.

◆ If you do not plan to install corner molding, trim the sharp corner with a block plane to prevent chipping.

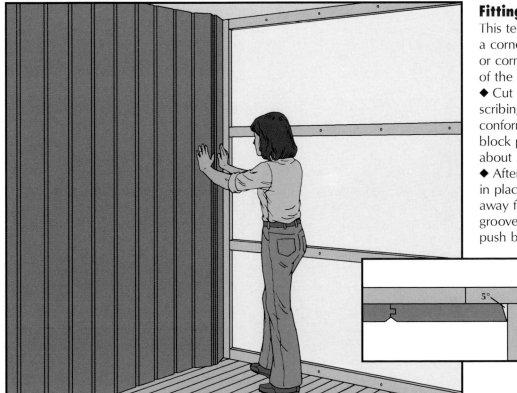

Fitting to an inside corner.

This technique is particularly helpful in a corner where no adjoining paneling or corner molding will cover the edge of the final board.

◆ Cut the final board exactly to width, scribing the cut edge, if necessary, to conform to the corner. Then use a block plane to bevel the corner edge about 5 degrees *(inset).*

◆ After locking the next-to-last board in place, pull its tongue edge slightly away from the wall, slip on the grooved edge of the final board, and push both boards against the wall at once *(left).*

◆ Nail the boards as shown in Step 3 on page 83.

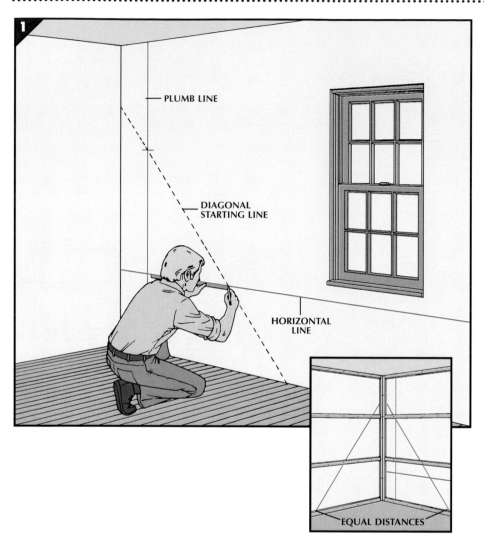

PLUMB LINE

DIAGONAL
STARTING LINE

HORIZONTAL
LINE

EQUAL DISTANCES

1. Laying out a 45-degree starting line.

Furring strips for a diagonal pattern are installed wall by wall, after each is marked with a diagonal starting line. Construct the line in the direction you want the boards to run, making sure it does not lap over a door or window.

◆ To begin, snap a plumb chalk line from ceiling to floor about 16 inches from the corner of the room, then snap a horizontal line across it about 2 feet from the floor.

◆ Mark each of the lines 3 feet from their intersection, and connect these points with a diagonal line. Extend the line to the corner and floor.

◆ Install furring strips on the wall *(page 80)*.

If the projected paneling reverses direction at a corner, forming an inverted V pattern, construct a second starting line based on the first.

◆ Measure from the corner to the bottom of the first starting line; then mark off this distance along the bottom of the adjoining wall.

◆ Snap a diagonal line between this mark and the top of the first starting line, then install furring strips *(inset)*.

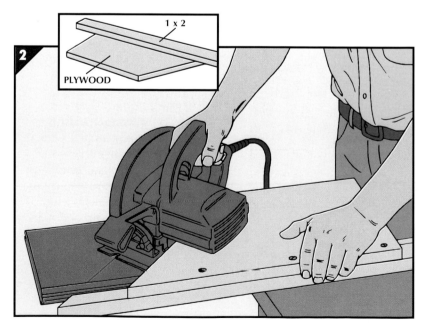

1 x 2

PLYWOOD

2. Cutting boards to fit.

Use a circular saw and a 45-degree jig that you can make from plywood and a 1-by-2 *(inset)* to miter each end of the board. Make sure that the miters match the surfaces that the board will abut—the floor, wall, ceiling, door, or window.

◆ To cut the first board, measure the length of the starting line.

◆ Transfer the measurement to the grooved edge of the board, then start the cuts at that edge *(left)*.

◆ To cut consecutive boards above the first, measure the length of the tongue edge on the previous board.

When more than one board length is needed for a long diagonal, cut the two board ends square. Apply glue and butt them together. Stagger these butted joints as you go up the wall so that they will not form a diagonal line across the wall.

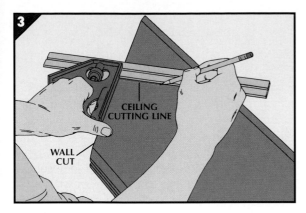

3. Measuring double-angle cuts.

◆ When the end of a board hits two surfaces perpendicular to each other—such as a wall and the ceiling *(below, middle board)*—first miter the end to fit against one of the surfaces (in this example, the wall).

◆ Measure how much of the wall corner remains to be covered by paneling, and mark off this distance on the mitered end, measuring from the grooved edge.

◆ Use a combination square to draw a perpendicular line from the mark to the tongue edge of the board *(left),* and make the second cut—here, the ceiling cut—along that line.

4. Maintaining a 45-degree angle.

Check the angle of the first three boards after you position each one.

◆ Hold a steel square against the board, lining up the two 12-inch marks on the square with the tongue edge of the board.

◆ Now place a carpenter's level on the horizontal arm of the square and adjust the board until the arm is level.

◆ Nail the board in place.

5. Flanking an opening with a diagonal.

◆ Where a board overlaps the corner of the window or door opening, tap it in place and check its angle *(Step 4, above).*

◆ Reach behind the board and mark the tongue edge at the inside edges of the furring strips that frame the corner.

◆ Remove the board, lay it facedown, and use a combination square to draw a 45-degree line across the board at each mark *(inset).*

◆ Cut out the resulting triangle with a saber saw, then nail the board in place.

COMPOUND MITER

WASTE END

◆ Remove the board and then clamp it, facedown, across two sawhorses. Set the blade of a circular saw at a 45-degree angle.
◆ Using a diagonal jig to guide the saw, cut along the marked line with the blade pointing toward the waste end of the board. Doing so creates a compound miter—an edge that is both mitered and beveled.
◆ Tap the board in place, with the compound miter extending beyond the corner *(inset)*, and nail it.

6. Fitting an outside corner.
◆ To install the first board that meets the corner of the wall, miter both ends and tap the board in place.
◆ At the bottom of the board, mark the part that extends beyond the corner by drawing a line across the back of the board *(above)*.

On subsequent boards, miter the top but leave the bottom end temporarily unmitered. Tap the board in place, mark the part that extends beyond the corner, then cut a compound miter along this line. At the top of the wall, where the last board is simply a small triangle, use wood glue as well as nails to help anchor the board to the furring.

7. Trimming lower boards for fit.
◆ Working down from the starting board, miter the boards to fit, but here use the grooved edge of the previous board as a measure.
◆ Before installing a shorter board near the bottom corner, chisel off the backside of the grooved edge to facilitate fitting the next board.
◆ Check the angle and nail the board in place.
◆ Anchor the triangular board at the base of the wall with wood glue as well as nails.

Turning an inside corner.
◆ Cut the first board for the second wall as in Step 2 on page 86, using the previously drawn starting line as a measure.
◆ Position the board so that it forms an inverted V with its mate.
◆ Cut and install succeeding boards, always taking care to match each board to its mate on the adjoining wall.

REFERENCE BOARD   EQUAL DISTANCES

WASTE END

Joining boards at an outside corner.
◆ Where a diagonal forms a V at an outside corner, choose a reference board on the paneled wall. Measure along the ceiling from the lower edge of the reference board to the corner of the room, and transfer the measurement to the adjacent wall. Then draw a starting line from that point to where the lower edge of the reference board meets the corner (inset).
◆ Install furring strips on this wall.
◆ Miter the ceiling end of a panel board that is a little longer than the reference board.
◆ Butt the board against the ceiling, and line up the other end with its mate on the adjoining wall. Have a helper hold the board at the starting line but slightly away from the wall—to allow for the protruding miter of its mate—and mark a cutting line on the back of the board (left). Transfer the cutting line to the front of the board.
◆ Clamp the board, faceup, across two sawhorses and set the circular saw at a 45-degree angle. Pointing the blade away from the waste end, use a diagonal jig to guide the saw one blade thickness outside the marked line to allow for trimming the final joint between the two boards.
◆ Once the joint fits, spread wood glue on the mitered end, and when the board is nailed in place, fasten the mitered ends together with brads.
◆ Mark, cut, and attach all the remaining boards as shown on pages 86 to 88.
◆ When all the boards are in place, use a block plane to smooth the sharp corner. You may omit this detail if you plan to install corner molding.

A HERRINGBONE DESIGN OF MITERED BOARDS

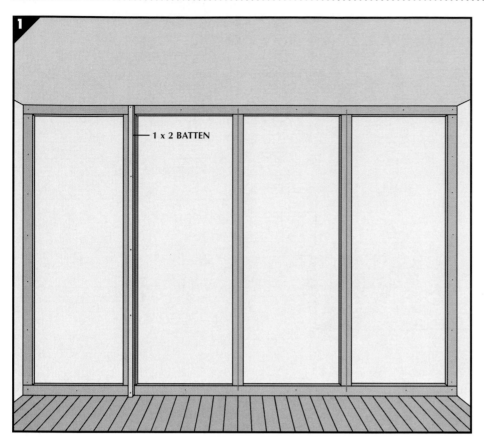

1 x 2 BATTEN

1. Installing the furring strips.

◆ With baseboard and ceiling molding removed, divide the wall vertically into equal parts, marking each division with a plumb chalk line.

◆ Frame the perimeter of the wall with 1-by-4 furring strips, then center and nail a furring strip over each chalked line. If vertical strips are not positioned over studs, attach the strips to the wallboard with construction adhesive. To hold a strip in place while the glue dries, drive two angled nails through it and into the wallboard every 16 inches or so *(page 93, inset)*.

◆ Snap a chalk line down the center of each strip.

◆ At the chalked line on the first furring strip, tack a temporary 1-by-2 batten as a guide for the mitered ends of the first section of boards. A straight batten works best, but you can bend a slightly curved batten to the chalked line as you tack it.

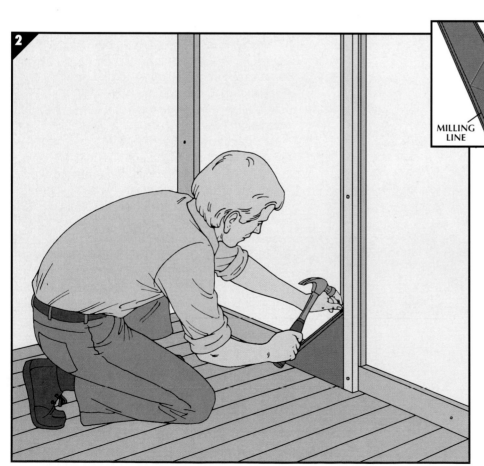

MILLING LINE

2. Attaching the first board.

◆ With the technique shown in the inset to Step 5 on page 87, mark cutting lines for a right triangle on a panel board, placing the right angle where the milling begins on the grooved edge of the board *(inset)*.

◆ Glue and nail the board in the corner formed by the floor and the batten.

Measure, cut, and install diagonal boards to complete the first wall section, using the methods described on pages 86 and 87.

3. Completing the herringbone.

◆ Remove the batten from the first furring strip, and tack it along the chalked line on the second furring strip.

◆ Install the next section of diagonal boards, beginning with a triangle as before but working from the opposite corner so the boards slope in the opposite direction. Make sure each board aligns perfectly against the corresponding board in the first section, to form a V.

◆ Move the batten to the third furring strip.

◆ Since the next section slopes upward, choose a reference board *(page 89, bottom)* in the second section to guide installation.

◆ Continue across the wall, using the methods on pages 88 to 90.

A CHOICE OF FINISHES FOR FINE WOOD

After filling nail holes, lightly sanding the wood, and cleaning away the dust with a damp cloth, you are ready to finish the walls. Most woods require some sort of finish to protect them from dirt and scratches. The materials you choose to finish the paneling depend on the time you wish to invest and the appearance you wish to achieve. Staining the wood before applying a finish, for example, is not necessary, but it enhances natural color and emphasizes grain. Choose a stain and a finish that are both either water-base or oil-base.

Water-base stains and polyurethane (the most durable) finishes are good for quick application and easy soap-and-water cleanup and are less toxic than oil-base products. Extra sanding is required (since the water in the stain tends to raise the woodgrain), but the finish is crystal clear. Oil-base staining is more time consuming but will dye the wood more deeply than most water-base products. Oil-base finish is also more toxic than water-base and will tend to yellow over time.

Apply water-base stain with a brush having nylon bristles, a foam brush, a pad applicator, or a rag. Allow the liquid to penetrate the wood for about 5 minutes, then wipe off the excess in the direction of the grain with a clean rag. Let the wood dry for about 2 hours before finishing.

When applying the finish, use the same brush or a pad applicator. Since water-base finishes dry quickly, it is important not to overbrush the finish; doing so leaves brush marks on the wood. After 3 to 4 hours, burnish the finish with plastic wool, then wipe with a dampened cloth. Apply at least one more coat.

To apply an oil-base stain, use a brush or pad applicator and leave the stain on the wood no more than 30 minutes. Wipe excess with a rag and let the wood dry for 12 hours before finishing. Oil-base polyurethane finishes, applied with a varnish brush, must dry for 12 to 24 hours between coats. Smooth with plastic wool between coats. Tools can be cleaned with turpentine or mineral spirits.

⚠ **CAUTION** *Make sure the room is well ventilated when applying oil-base stains and finishes and extinguish any nearby flames. Enclose oily rags in an airtight, flameproof can for disposal.*

Raised paneling, perfected in Colonial times, will lend elegance to any room. With the proper tools, you can make and install the traditional solid-wood version. Or, to save time and money, you can create a facsimile by adding stiles, rails, and other embellishments to plywood panels.

Making a Pattern: Planning is crucial with either type. First make a scale drawing of the existing walls, showing door and window openings, electric switches and outlets, and any other protruding fixtures. Then superimpose a sketch of the paneling on this drawing.

Panel widths should not exceed 24 inches, except at doors and windows, where they should be wide enough to span the opening. Plan the layout so each hole for an electric switch or outlet will fall on a flat surface, rather than on a joint or a section of molding; you may have to move electrical elements. For frame-on-plywood paneling, position stiles to cover the joints between plywood panels.

The width of stiles, rails, and moldings depends on the proportions of the wall but should fall within a general range—stiles, 4 to 6 inches; rails, $2\frac{1}{2}$ to $3\frac{1}{2}$ inches; base moldings, $3\frac{1}{2}$ to 5 inches; crown moldings, 3 inches; door and window casings, 3 inches. Refine your sketch to include these dimensions, then transfer your pattern directly to the wall.

Construction: For frame-on-plywood paneling, use furniture-grade $\frac{1}{4}$-inch plywood, and assemble the paneling directly on the wall. Finishing or painting the paneling and the rails, stiles, and embellishments before installing usually produces a neater finished product. If you are attaching the pieces to the wall with adhesive, however, leave bare all the areas to be glued for better adhesion, and touch up the finish after installation.

For solid-wood raised paneling, softwoods work best. Assemble cut pieces and fasten them to the wall in completed upper-and-lower sections *(page 99),* applying the finish after installation. See page 91 for suggested finishes for solid-wood paneling. You can also finish solid-wood paneling with paint.

TOOLS

Table saw	Router
Carpenter's level	Combination square
Miter box	Dovetail saw
Mallet	Wood chisel
Nail set	Doweling jig
Dado head	Electric drill
C-clamps	Dowel centers
	Pipe clamps
	Block plane

MATERIALS

Boards ($\frac{3}{4}$")	Wood putty
Plywood ($\frac{1}{4}$")	Hardboard ($\frac{1}{8}$")
Finishing nails ($2\frac{1}{2}$", 3")	2 x 4s, 1 x 6s, 1 x 2s
Construction adhesive	Carpenter's glue
Moldings	Sandpaper
Brads ($\frac{3}{4}$" and 1")	Flat-head stove bolts
	Fluted dowels

SAFETY TIPS

When hammering or drilling, wear safety glasses to protect your eyes from flying nails or woodchips.

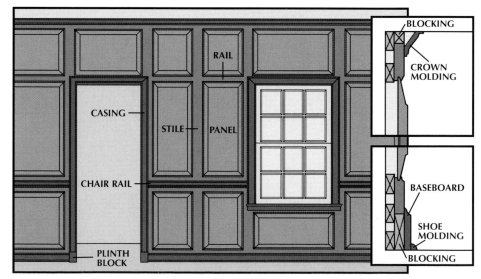

The parts of a raised panel wall.

Vertical stiles and horizontal rails, made of $\frac{3}{4}$-inch boards and joined together with glued dowels, hold the panels inside grooved edges. The top and bottom rails rest against blocking made of inexpensive $\frac{3}{4}$-inch lumber that is slightly narrower than the molding that covers it *(insets).* Each assembled section is nailed to furring strips behind the edges of every rail and the blocking.

Crown molding trims the wall at the ceiling; casings border the doors and windows. Chair-rail molding covers a joint between upper and lower frame sections, and baseboard and shoe molding separates wall and floor. On both sides of the door, rectangular plinth blocks fill the corner between the casing and base molding.

A FACSIMILE WITH PLYWOOD

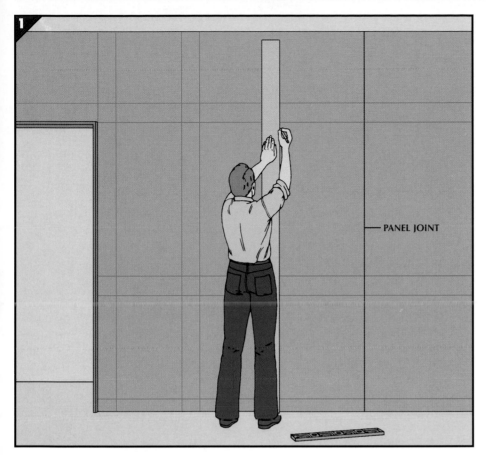

1. **Laying out the frame.**
◆ Panel the walls with $\frac{1}{4}$-inch plywood as shown on pages 66 to 73; if you are using furring strips, add horizontal ones at the rail heights.
◆ With a pencil and a long straight-edged board, mark positions for the edges of stiles and rails on the plywood-paneled wall. Make sure that all joints between the plywood panels will be covered by stiles and that no stile or rail edge will cross an electrical outlet or switch.
◆ Mark the location of the bottom edge of the bottom rail; it should be 1 inch lower than the top edge of the planned base molding.
◆ Finally, cut all of the stiles, making them $\frac{1}{2}$ inch shorter than the overall wall height for ease in installation.

PANEL JOINT

2. **Attaching the stiles and rails.**
◆ Line up a stile with one set of stile-edge marks; check it with a carpenter's level for plumb.
◆ If the paneling is installed over furring strips, nail the stile through the paneling to the strips with 3-inch finishing nails; use two at each strip (*left*).
◆ Position, level, and nail the rest.
◆ Measure and cut rails for a snug fit between stiles, using a miter box to ensure perfectly square ends.
◆ Line up the rails with the pencil marks and tap them into position with a mallet, placing a wood block between mallet and rail.
◆ Nail the rails in place.

If the paneling is installed on wallboard, attach the stiles to the paneling with construction adhesive. Then angle two $2\frac{1}{2}$-inch finishing nails through the stiles into the wall at each rail height to keep stiles in place until the adhesive sets (*inset*). Measure and cut the rails as above, then glue and nail them into place.

3. Adding mitered molding.
◆ To finish the edges of stiles and rails with quarter-round or patterned molding, cut molding to the length of the rail or stile edge to be covered, and miter each molding end inward at a 45-degree angle *(page 39)*.
◆ Nail the molding in place with 1-inch brads, starting with a stile and working clockwise around to the remaining three sides of the rectangle.
◆ Repeat for each frame, then fill any cracks at miter joints with wood putty.

4. Adding embellishments.
◆ For a raised-panel effect in the rectangle *(below, left),* cut a piece of $\frac{1}{8}$-inch hardboard 2 inches shorter and narrower than the inside measure of the rectangle.
◆ Bevel the panel's edges with a table saw, then center it in the rectangle and attach it with glue and $\frac{3}{4}$-inch brads.
◆ Repeat for the other rectangles.

Alternatively, add a molding rectangle of the same dimensions as the raised panel described above *(below, right).*

◆ Outline its location in pencil, then use the technique described in Step 3 to nail the mitered molding along the outline.
◆ Repeat for the other rectangles.
◆ Countersink all nails and fill holes with wood putty.

A FRAME FOR SOLID-WOOD PANELS

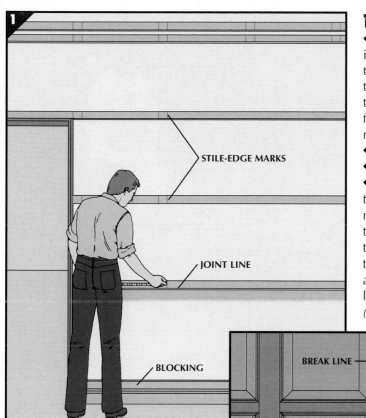

STILE-EDGE MARKS

JOINT LINE

BLOCKING

BREAK LINE

1. Laying out the frame.

◆ Nail furring strips to the wall along the floor and the ceiling, at each rail level, and at the midpoint between any rails that will be more than 2 feet apart *(pages 21-24)*. Determine the location of the joint between the upper and lower sections of the wall. (It will be concealed by the chair rail.) The furring strip there must be doubled or wide enough that each rail edge is backed by furring.
◆ Nail blocking over the furring strip at floor level *(page 92)*.
◆ Mark the exact positions of stile edges on all the strips.
◆ Calculate the exact stile, rail, and panel dimensions using the stile-edge marks. Stiles for the lower section of panels reach from the top of the blocking to the joint line; stiles for the upper section reach from the joint line to 2 inches below the ceiling. Measure the distance between stile edges to determine rail lengths. If you plan to shape the edges of stiles and rails, allow for the decorative edge in calculating the length of the rail, which must meet the stile at the break line *(inset)* where the shaped edge begins.
◆ Cut the stiles and rails, lay them facedown on the floor in the relative positions they will occupy on the wall, and mark them with matching numbers at each joint to speed later assembly.

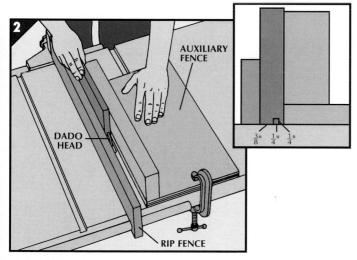

AUXILIARY FENCE

DADO HEAD

RIP FENCE

$\frac{3}{8}$" $\frac{1}{4}$" $\frac{1}{4}$"

2. Cutting grooves in rails and stiles.

◆ Install a $\frac{1}{4}$-inch dado head on the table saw and lock the rip fence $\frac{3}{8}$ inch from the blade.
◆ Clamp an auxiliary fence—a 2-by-4 nailed to a piece of plywood—to the saw table on the other side of the blade, separated from the rip fence by the thickness of the lumber used for stiles and rails.
◆ Set the dado head to cut $\frac{1}{4}$ inch above the table. With the power on, feed rails and stiles—one edge down and the outside face against the rip fence—over the dado head.

MAKING SKILLFUL CUTS

A featherboard serves as an excellent alternative to the auxiliary fence shown at left, especially when you are working with flawed wood. Not only does the featherboard keep your workpiece from shifting or kicking back as it moves over the table-saw blade, its springy feathers also flex with any warps or imperfections in the wood.

To make a featherboard, miter-cut a 60-degree angle at the end of a 1-by-3 hardwood board. Then make parallel cuts about 5 inches long and $\frac{1}{4}$ inch apart into the mitered end. To use the featherboard, clamp it to the saw table with the feathers touching the workpiece, keeping the wood pressed snugly against the fence.

FEATHERBOARD

3. Shaping stile and rail edges.

◆ Clamp a stile, faceup, on a worktable and put the desired edge-forming bit in the router.

◆ Rest the router base on the stile with the bit an inch or so in from one end; turn on the router and push it toward the stile until the pilot comes into contact with the edge of the wood *(inset)*.

◆ Slowly move the router to the near end of the stile until the bit clears the corner, then move it in the opposite direction, shaping the entire edge of the stile.

◆ If the clamp blocks the path of the router, switch off the motor, reposition the clamp, and restart the cut an inch away from the stopping point, bringing the pilot against the still-uncut edge of the stile.

◆ Shape the stile's opposite edge in the same way; repeat the shaping process on all the remaining stiles and rails except along those edges that are going to be covered by chair-rail molding, door casing, or base molding.

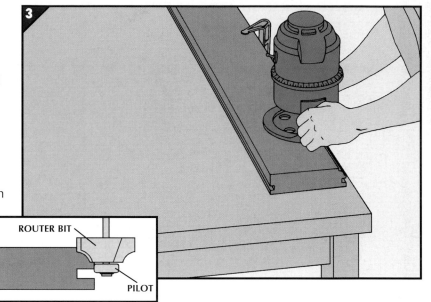

ROUTER BIT

PILOT

4. Preparing a shaped stile for joints.

◆ On the back of a stile that has a shaped edge, mark the points where the rail edges will intersect the stile.

◆ Use a combination square to mark the converging lines of a 45-degree angle from these points *(below, left)*.

◆ With a dovetail saw or other fine-tooth saw, cut along the lines down to the break line of the shaped edge *(below, right)*.

◆ Using a wood chisel with the beveled edge facing down, remove the wood between the saw cuts. Chisel off chips about $\frac{3}{4}$ inch long and $\frac{1}{16}$ inch thick until you have a flat surface at the level of the break line.

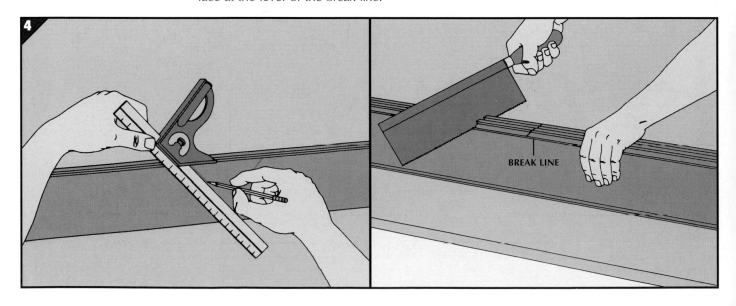

BREAK LINE

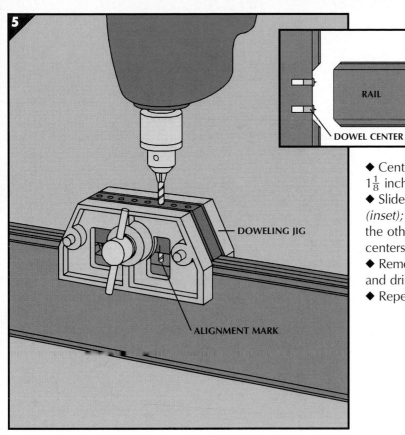

5. Drilling holes for dowels.

◆ Using a miter box, cut a 45-degree angle across each corner of the matching rail. Position the rail for the cut by aligning the saw blade over the point where the break line intersects the rail end.

◆ Mark guidelines for a doweling jig by drawing lines across both ends of the cutout section of a stile, $\frac{1}{2}$ inch in from the bottom of the bevel.

◆ Center the jig over each line and drill a $\frac{5}{16}$-inch hole, $1\frac{1}{8}$ inches deep.

◆ Slide a $\frac{5}{16}$-inch metal dowel center into each of the holes *(inset)*; fit the matching rail into the cutout section and tap the other end of the rail to force the points of the dowel centers into the wood.

◆ Remove the rail, align the jig over the dowel-center marks, and drill holes in the rail end to match those in the stile.

◆ Repeat Steps 4 and 5 wherever rails and stiles intersect.

MAKING THE RAISED PANELS

1. Joining boards edge-to-edge.

◆ Select several $\frac{3}{4}$-inch-thick boards that are long enough to make one or two raised panel sections and have a combined width that is greater than the planned width of one panel.

◆ Alternating the direction of the grain to prevent warping, lay the boards edge-to-edge across pipe clamps posi-tioned near the board ends and at 2- to 3-foot intervals in between.

◆ Place additional clamps across the tops of the boards parallel to and mid-way between those on the bottom.

◆ Tighten all the clamps, increasing the pressure evenly until the seams between boards are nearly invisible hairlines.

◆ If there are gaps between the boards, remove the clamps and shave the board edges with a block plane.

◆ When board edges meet evenly, spread carpenter's glue on each board edge and reclamp the boards.

◆ After the glue is dry, remove the clamps, cut the panels to size, and sand the faces.

2. Outlining the bevel.

◆ Set the cutting height of a table-saw blade at $\frac{1}{16}$ inch and position the rip fence 2 inches from the blade.

◆ Hold a panel facedown, one edge against the rip fence, and make a $\frac{1}{16}$-inch-deep cut down the length of the panel face. Repeat the same cut on the other three edges of the panel.

◆ Outline the bevels for all the panels, and make similar cuts on a piece of scrap wood the same thickness as the panels, to use in setting the saw blade for the bevel cut.

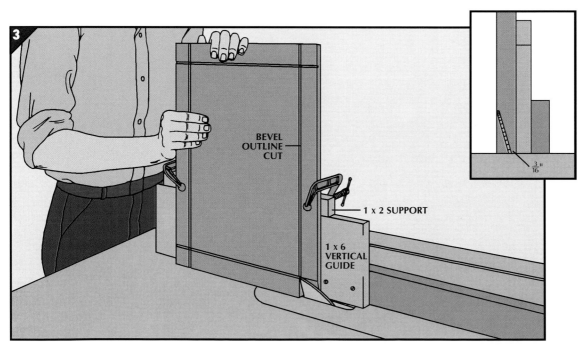

BEVEL OUTLINE CUT

1 x 2 SUPPORT

1 x 6 VERTICAL GUIDE

$\frac{3}{16}$"

3. Cutting the bevel.

◆ Tilt the saw blade away from the rip fence at a 15-degree angle, and fasten a 1-by-6 board to the rip fence as a guide. Anchor the guide to the fence with countersunk flat-head stove bolts.

◆ Position the guide so that its face is $\frac{3}{16}$ inch away from the saw blade at table level, and adjust the cutting height of the blade so that its highest part reaches exactly to the bevel outline you have cut on the piece of scrap lumber *(inset)*.

◆ Slide a panel into the space between the blade and the guide, with the back of the panel against the guide and the end grain down.

◆ To steady the panel, rest a length of 1-by-2 on top of the guide and clamp the panel and the 1-by-2 together.

◆ Turn on the saw and, keeping your hands well above the table, push the panel over the blade.

◆ Repeat this procedure on each side of the panel, repositioning and reclamping the 1-by-2 support before each cut.

◆ Repeat for each panel.

FINAL ASSEMBLY AND INSTALLATION

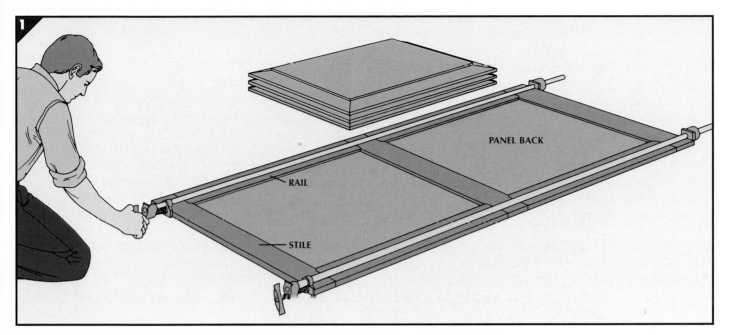

RAIL

PANEL BACK

STILE

1. Joining the parts.
◆ Place the panels, rails, and stiles of the lower paneling section facedown on the floor, with the adjoining edges facing each other and the bottom edge toward the wall.
◆ Using a wood mallet, tap 2-inch-long fluted dowels into all of the rail holes; then tap the panels into the rail grooves; finally, tap the stiles onto the dowels protruding from the rails.

◆ After successfully test-fitting the pieces, disassemble them and spread a thin film of carpenter's glue inside the dowel holes and on all the facing edges of the joints, but not in the grooves.
◆ Reassemble the parts, using pipe clamps stretched from stile to stile to close the joints.
◆ Let the glue dry, remove the clamps, and assemble the remaining sections in the same way.

BLOCKING

2. Raising the paneling.
◆ With helpers providing support at each stile, tilt the lower paneling section against the wall, then lift it and set the bottom rail on the blocking.
◆ Slide a level along the top of the paneling while a helper wedges thin wood shims between the blocking and the bottom rail to level the section.
◆ Fasten the stiles to the wall at each furring strip with pairs of $2\frac{1}{2}$ inch finishing nails.
◆ Raise the upper paneling section into position on top of the lower one, aligning the stiles exactly, and nail the upper stiles to the furring strips.
◆ Nail blocking between the top rail and the ceiling.
◆ When all of the sections are in place, cover the joint between the upper and lower sections with chair rail, and add ceiling, corner, and base moldings *(pages 78-79 and 92)*.
◆ Frame the door and window openings with casings that match the wood of the stiles and rails.
◆ Countersink all nails with a nail set, and fill the holes with wood putty.

The Classic Look of Wainscoting

Not all wall paneling rises from floor to ceiling; a traditional variety known as wainscoting stops at about hip level. Wainscot paneling can vary in height from 30 to 36 inches, but it generally looks best when it is no more than one-third the height of the wall.

Wainscoting can be made from any of the materials—and in any of the styles—described earlier in this chapter. Wainscoting kits are also available at home centers and lumberyards.

Molding for a Neat Finish: As with floor-to-ceiling paneling, regular baseboard and shoe molding serve as trim at the floor. Wainscoting differs from full-height panels only in the molding that covers the upper edge. You can employ one-piece cap molding as the top trim for thin wainscoting *(below, left)*. Thicker panels, or ones nailed to furring strips, require wider and more elaborate assemblies of three different pieces of molding *(below, right)*.

Outside corners of the trim are ordinarily mitered or square cut. At inside corners, you can ensure a better fit with a coping cut *(opposite)*. If you plan to set the top molding at the same height as the window stool (the inside extension of the window sill), you will need to scribe and then cut the top molding in much the same fashion as that outlined on page 76.

 TOOLS

Hammer
Miter box and backsaw
Coping saw

 **MATERIALS**

Plywood (interior, $\frac{1}{4}$")
Wood panels
Cap molding
Window-stool stock

Cove molding
Base-cap molding
Baseboard
Shoe molding
Bright finishing nails

SUITING THE MOLDING TO THE PANELS

Top trim for thin wainscoting.
For $\frac{1}{4}$-inch plywood or sheet paneling fastened directly to the wall, the easiest trim to apply is cap molding, already factory cut to lap over the panel edge.

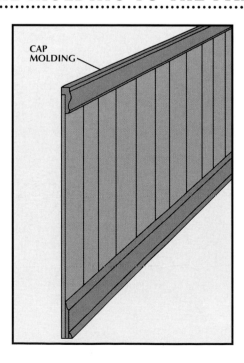

CAP MOLDING

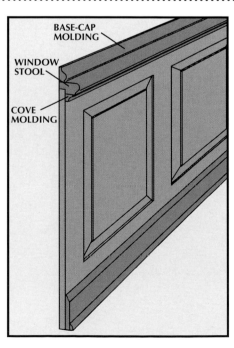

BASE-CAP MOLDING
WINDOW STOOL
COVE MOLDING

Complex molding for thicker panels.
If paneling protrudes farther than the depth of the cap molding—generally $\frac{1}{4}$ inch—you can use window-stool stock, rip cut to the desired width. Trim the stool stock with base-cap molding above and cove molding below.

A COPED JOINT FOR CAP MOLDING

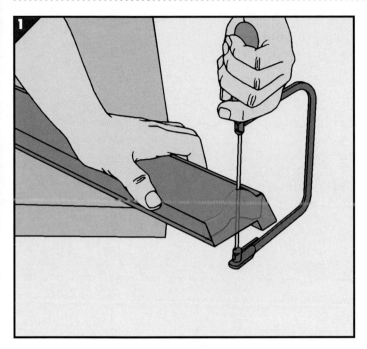

1. Shaping the first piece.
◆ When two pieces of cap molding meet at an inside corner, miter the end of the first piece.
◆ Outline the contoured edge in pencil as shown on page 78, then continue the pencil line across the top of the molding at right angles to the back edge.
◆ With a coping saw, make a vertical cut through the molding along this line *(left)*.

2. Cutting the second piece.
◆ Notch another piece of molding *(right)* to the depth of the wainscot paneling.
◆ Nail that piece to the wall.
◆ Slide the first piece against it *(inset)* and nail it in place.

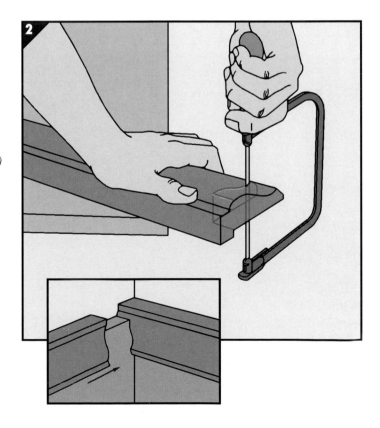

Improvements in Form and Function

4 Ordinary rooms lend themselves to alteration for purely personal needs—from suspended ceilings of sound-absorbing acoustic panels and banks of indirect lighting, to the cosmetic effect of false beams. One useful modification is muting intrusive noise with doubled wall surfaces and extra layers of insulation. A sense of security comes from safeguarding valuables in a hollow wall or above a false ceiling.

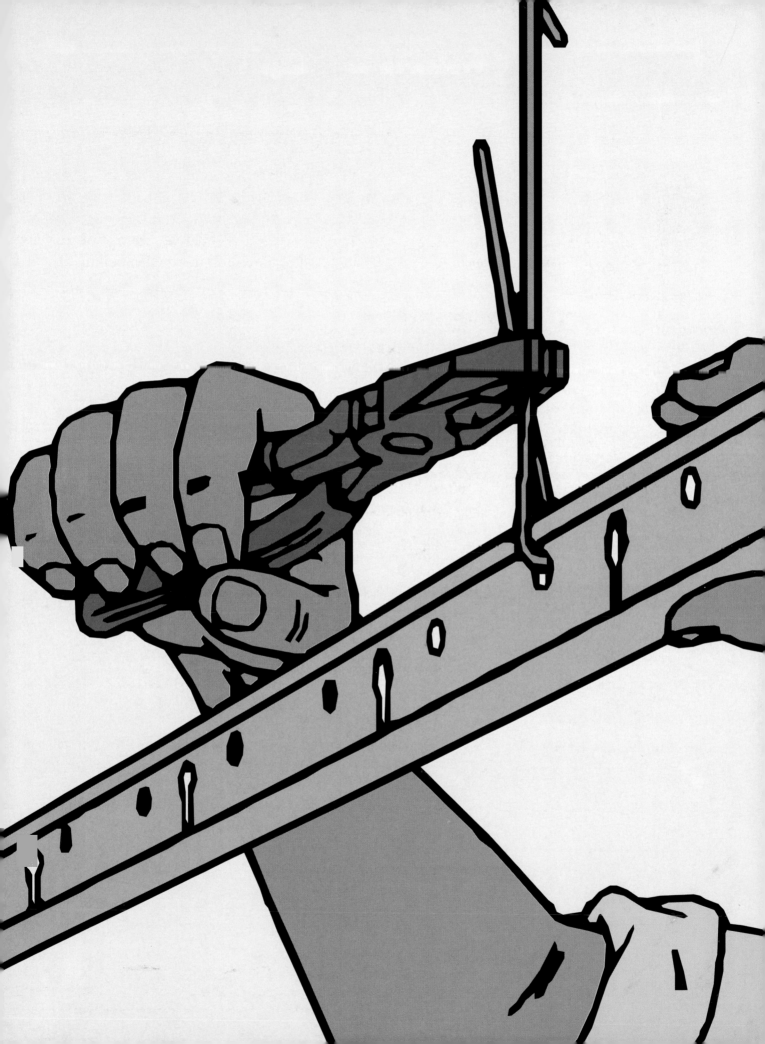

Prefabricated Ceilings

Aprefabricated ceiling, easy to install and designed to absorb sound, can be an appealing alternative to plaster or wallboard. Two basic structural systems are used for such ceilings: interlocking tiles that are attached to the old ceiling *(right and pages 105-107)* or floating panels suspended from the old ceiling on a lightweight metal grid *(pages 108-111)*. Because the tiles or panels of a prefabricated ceiling are precut and already embossed with a decorative finish, they dispense with such plaster or wallboard preliminaries as mortar mixing or joint taping as well as a final application of paint or wallpaper. As for their acoustic benefits, they can absorb 50 to 80 percent of the sound that would otherwise reverberate in a room.

Tile Ceilings: The installation method for tiles depends on the condition of the existing ceiling. If your ceiling is level and free of cracks, you can fasten tiles directly to the existing surface with brush-on adhesive and staples (first removing any loose paint or wallpaper). If, however, the ceiling is cracked or uneven, an intermediate buffer of furring strips *(right)* will be needed.

You can hide obstructions, such as a pipe or duct, by building a wood frame around the obstacle *(pages 25-26),* then fastening tiles to the frames.

Suspended Ceilings: When a number of overhead pipes or ducts must be concealed—as in an unfinished basement, for instance—a ceiling made of suspended panels is the logical choice. Better lighting may be another reason: Fluorescent-light fixtures set into the grid flush with the ceiling provide a more even light than narrow surface-mounted fixtures. To provide the maximum amount of light reflection, paint the existing ceiling structure above the fixtures—including any exposed joists—with two coats of vinyl-base, nonyellowing white paint.

First Steps: Acoustic tiles and panels should be unpacked and allowed to stand for at least 24 hours in the room where they are to be installed. This allows them to become acclimated to the temperature and humidity. You should also complete electrical wiring for the ceiling before installing tiles or panel grids *(pages 27 and 110).*

CLIP-ON TILES

In the case of a cracked or uneven ceiling, tiles must be attached to furring strips for support. The strips can be made either of wood *(pages 21-24)* or of metal. Wood is less expensive, but the metal system eliminates the need to staple each tile in place. Instead, tiles are secured with metal clips, which come in a kit with the furring strips. The clips snap onto each strip and hook over one of the tile's flange edges *(above).*

Metal strips are laid out in the same way as wood strips *(opposite),* except that a final strip is placed an inch from the edge of each wall that runs perpendicular to the joists. Several strips compose one row, with a slight gap, no wider than $\frac{1}{4}$ inch, between each strip. The strips must be perfectly aligned in case a clip needs to straddle two of them. If a full-length strip is too long to finish a row, cut it to size.

 TOOLS

Steel rule
Chalk line
Hammer
Staple gun
Utility knife
Compass

L square
Line level
Saw (keyhole or
   saber-saw blade)
Hacksaw
Tin snips
Pop riveter
Punch or drill

 MATERIALS

Acoustic ceiling
  tiles
Acoustic ceiling
  panels
Luminous panel
Furring strips
Cove molding
L-shaped wall
  angles
Runners
Cross Ts

Channel molding
Vertical cross Ts
Hanger wires
Ceiling staples
Common nails ($1\frac{1}{2}$")
Finishing nails ($2\frac{1}{2}$")
Dry-wall nails or
  screws ($1\frac{1}{4}$")
Screw eyes
Rivets
Cable connector
Lock nut
Wire caps

 SAFETY TIPS

Protect your eyes with goggles when stapling, sawing, hammering, and riveting. Wear both goggles and gloves when cutting metal.

STAPLING CEILING TILE TO FURRING STRIPS

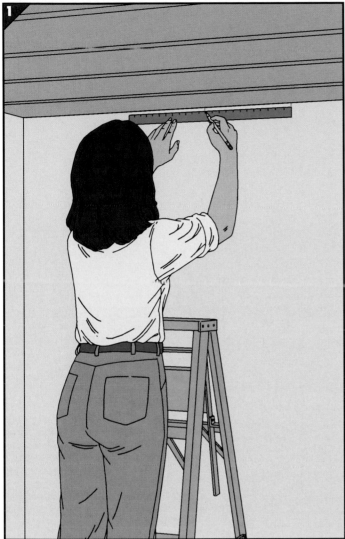

1. Laying out the work.

The following method of planning the installation of 1-foot-square ceiling tiles ensures borders of equal and visually pleasing width. A graph paper map of the layout can be useful.

◆ Find the midpoint of a wall and measure from there to the corner. If the distance is an even number of feet plus 3 inches or more, use the midpoint as the starting point in marking off 1-foot intervals along the top of the wall *(left)*. If less than 3 inches, move the starting point 6 inches to the left or right of the midpoint. Mark all walls in this way, and mark the location of any concealed joists *(page 8)*.

◆ To calculate the quantity of tiles needed, count the 1-foot intervals along two adjacent walls; add 1 to each number, then multiply the two numbers.

◆ To determine the quantity of furring strips, count the 1-foot intervals along one of the walls that parallel the joists, and add 2 to this number.

◆ Snap a chalk line across the ceiling between corresponding marks on the two walls running parallel to the joists.

◆ Center furring strips over these lines, and nail them to the joists they cross, leveling them as shown on page 23, Step 3.

◆ Attach furring strips to the two ceiling edges that abut the joists.

2. Installing full tiles.

Use a hand or power stapler *(photograph)* for installation.

◆ Start the tiling in one corner, using two chalk lines as guides. Snap one down the center of the next-to-last furring strip from the corner. Snap the other at a right angle to it, connecting the last pair of 1-foot marks on the walls that parallel the furring strips.

◆ Align the first full tile with the intersection of these lines, tongued edges facing the corner and grooved edges facing the center of the room.

◆ Staple through the flanges on the grooved edges and into the furring strips *(right)*.

◆ Slide two additional tiles into place, fitting their tongued edges into the grooved edges of the first tile *(inset)*. Make sure the grooved sides of each new tile face toward the positions of the next tiles.

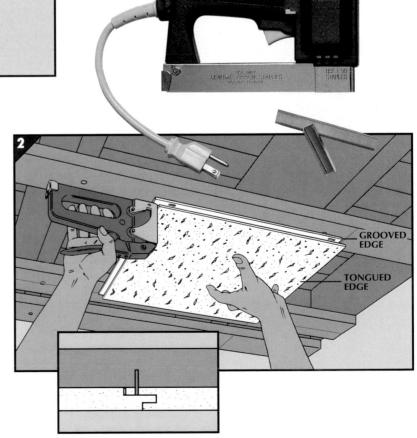

GROOVED EDGE

TONGUED EDGE

3. Adding border tiles.

To cut a border tile to size, measure the distance from both ends of the nearest full tile to the wall, transfer these measurements to a tile, and cut the tile with a utility knife and a straightedge guide *(left)*. Start a border at a corner as follows:

◆ Temporarily slide the border tiles on either side of a corner into place, with their cut edges against the wall.

◆ Using the two border tiles as a guide, measure and cut the corner tile. Then remove the adjacent border tiles and insert the corner tile.

◆ Staple the flange edges of the corner tile to furring strips. Replace and staple the adjacent border tiles.

◆ Along the edges against the walls, fasten all the tiles with $1\frac{1}{2}$-inch common nails, which will be covered later by molding.

◆ Continue working outward in both directions from the corner, alternately installing full tiles and border tiles.

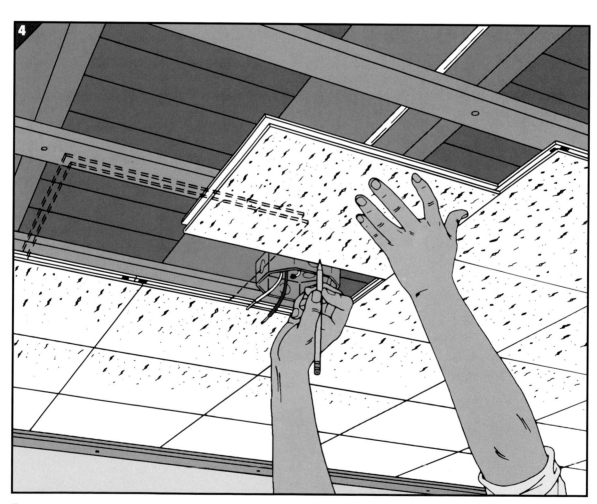

4. Marking an opening for an outlet box.

◆ Tile as closely as possible to two adjacent sides of an octagonal outlet or junction box.

◆ Slip the tongue of a free tile into the groove of an installed tile.

◆ Slide the free tile toward the outlet box until it butts against the edge. Lightly mark where the midpoint of the box meets the tile, then repeat the process on the adjacent side *(above)*.

◆ With a small L square, indicate the point where lines aligned with the two edge marks intersect; this marks the box's center.

◆ Use a compass to swing from this center a circle slightly smaller than the size of the box.

5. Cutting the box opening.
◆ With a keyhole or saber-saw blade angled slightly outward, cut a beveled edge around the marked circle.
◆ Slide the tile over the outlet box and staple it to the furring strips.
◆ Continue tiling outward until the entire ceiling is covered.

6. Attaching ceiling molding.
Cover the edges of the tile and the nailheads along the wall with $1\frac{1}{2}$-inch cove molding. For long strips of molding, have a helper steady one end while you attach the other *(left)*.
◆ Drive finishing nails through the center of the molding into the wall studs—$2\frac{1}{2}$-inch nails are generally sufficient, but use longer nails for heavier molding.
◆ Trim the molding so it will join snugly at the corners, using the techniques shown on page 79.

1. Installing the edge framing.

The framing at the edge of a suspended ceiling of 2- by 4-inch acoustic panels must be perfectly level; one leveling method uses chalk lines:

◆ Mark a corner at the desired ceiling height—at least 3 inches below any obstructions—and drive a nail in halfway. Stretch a chalk line from the nail to the next corner, hook a line level over it, and fasten the other end of the line in the corner when it is level. Remove the line level and snap the line against the wall. Repeat the process around the room.

◆ Secure L-shaped edge-framing strips to each wall with 1¼-inch dry-wall nails or screws driven into the studs. Position this framing with the long leg of the L against the wall and the other flush with the chalked line (left).

◆ Lap the ends of adjoining sections over one another (inset).

LASER LEVEL

A laser level, usually mounted on a tripod and placed in the center of a room, is topped with a rotating head that projects a reference line on the walls to aid in establishing ceiling height. This high-tech timesaver is available from rental centers.

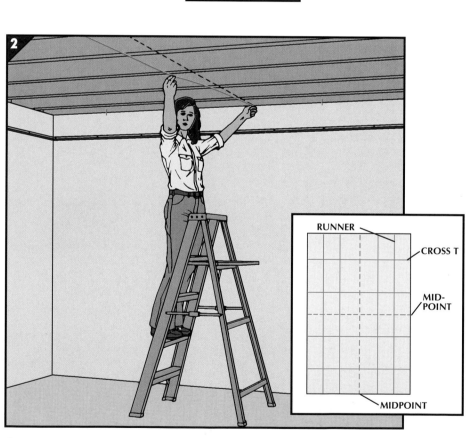

RUNNER
CROSS T
MID-POINT
MIDPOINT

2. Laying out the grid.

To establish the positions of runners and cross Ts (inset) supporting the panels, first mark the locations of any concealed joists (page 8), then proceed as follows:

◆ On walls parallel to the joists, mark the midpoint at joist level. On walls that run perpendicular to the joists, mark the midpoint just below the edge framing.

◆ Indicate positions for runners by snapping chalk lines at 2-foot intervals across the ceiling or exposed joists, at right angles to the joists. To determine the first runner position, calculate the overage by measuring the number of full feet from the midpoint of the wall to a corner (page 105, Step 1). If the overage is 6 inches or more, use the midpoint for the first runner position. If it is less than 6 inches, place the first runner 1 foot on either side of the midpoint, and use this position as a reference point for the other chalked lines.

◆ To lay out the positions for cross Ts, stretch strings across the ceiling at 4-foot intervals, parallel to the joists and attached just below the edge framing; check strings with a line level. Determine the position for the first cross T by measuring from a midpoint to a corner to find the overage, but this time note that the overage is calculated from the last foot mark divisible by 4. If the overage is 6 inches or more, stretch the first string between the midpoints; if it is less than 6 inches, offset the first string 2 feet to one side of the midpoints and use this string as a reference for the remaining strings.

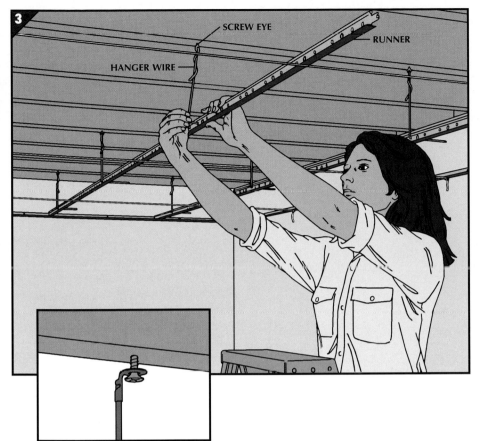

SCREW EYE

RUNNER

HANGER WIRE

3. Attaching the runners.

Use the stretched strings as guides to the height of the runners, checking frequently to make sure they are level.

◆ Position the runners so a slotted hole falls at every string line; trim the runners with a hacksaw when necessary.

◆ Working along the chalked lines, drive a screw eye into every fourth joist and suspend a hanger wire from it, allowing the wire to extend at least 6 inches below final ceiling height. Slip the wire through the nearest round hole of a runner, then twist it closed.

◆ To join sections of runners, butt or snap their ends together, according to their design. Make sure that slots in the added section align with the strings.

◆ Trim the runner ends to rest on the edge framing.

Some hanger wires are made with eyelets that loop over screws *(inset)*. To level the runner, simply adjust the screws.

4. Connecting the cross Ts.

◆ Hook the cross Ts into the runner slots every 2 feet at the locations marked by the strings.

◆ Trim the wall ends of the cross Ts with tin snips to rest squarely on the edge framing.

CROSS T

5. Installing a luminous panel.

◆ With the power turned off, run an electric cable from a junction box to where you will install the luminous panel.

◆ Insert four screw eyes into the joists above the location chosen for the luminous panel. Set the screws so the wire hangers will be angled slightly inward when attached to the panel.

◆ With a helper, angle the panel into position *(left)*, resting it on the flanged edges of the runners and the crossed Ts.

◆ Attach the top of the luminous panel to the four screw eyes with hanger wire threaded through prepunched holes in the panel.

◆ Once the panel is attached to the ceiling, follow the manufacturer's instructions to connect the wiring.

◆ Insert fluorescent tubes, close the outside cover, and turn on the power.

◆ Surround the luminous panel with acoustic panels, angled into position in the same way.

◆ At the edges of the ceiling, trim border panels to fit.

BOXING IN OBSTRUCTIONS

MAIN RUNNER

MAIN RUNNER

DROPPED RUNNER

DROPPED RUNNER

EDGE FRAMING

1. Installing a dropped runner.

When an obstruction runs parallel to the runners on the main part of the ceiling, install the main grid *(pages 108-109 and above)* as close as possible to both sides.

◆ Attach hanger wires directly beneath the last main runner on both sides of the obstruction, cutting the wires so the dropped runners will lie at least 3 inches below the obstruction. If the dropped runners butt against a wall, attach a piece of edge framing to the wall for support.

◆ Attach the runners to the hanger wires *(page 109, Step 3)*, aligning the slots for the cross Ts *(left)*.

If an obstruction runs perpendicular to the runners on the main ceiling, cut the main runners on both sides of the obstruction, leaving a 2-foot gap between them for cross Ts. Then install dropped runners as described above.

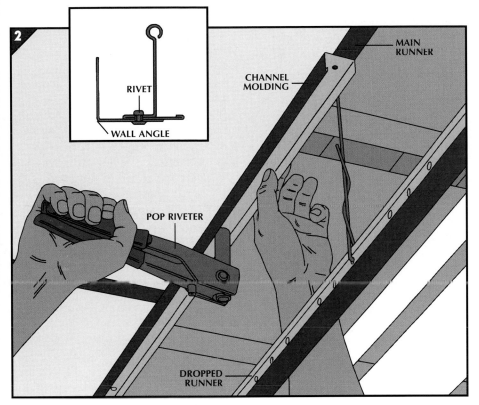

2. Attaching side-panel supports.
◆ Hold a piece of U-shaped channel molding against the bottom of the main runner nearest the obstruction and drill $\frac{3}{16}$-inch holes through both the molding and the runner's inner edge. Space the holes about 18 to 24 inches apart.
◆ Use a pop riveter to fasten the molding to the runner *(left)*.
◆ Fashion a support for the bottom of the side panels by fastening an L-shaped wall angle to the dropped runners, positioning it so that the space between the runner and the angle is just wide enough to accommodate the panel—usually $\frac{1}{2}$ to $\frac{3}{4}$ inch *(inset)*.
◆ If the enclosure does not extend all the way across the room, provide similar top and bottom supports for the panel that frames the end of the enclosure.

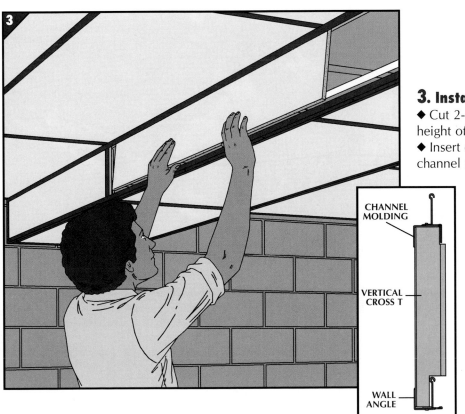

3. Installing side panels.
◆ Cut 2- by 4-foot acoustic panels to fit the height of the enclosure.
◆ Insert each panel by angling it up into the channel molding then letting it drop into the wall angle.
◆ As each panel is installed, add a vertical cross T to fit snugly between the wall angle on the dropped runner and the channel molding on the ceiling runner *(inset)*. Then insert another panel and continue in this way until the obstruction is enclosed. If the vertical cross Ts need steadying, you can pop rivet or screw them to the runners.

To provide a neat corner trim on an enclosure that does not extend across the room, fit sections of wall angle over the corner and attach the molding to the upper and lower runners.

Simulating a Beamed Ceiling

Exposed ceiling beams lend a room the aura of antiquity, but adding such beams requires major structural changes and the chore of hoisting heavy timbers. You can achieve the same look by creating lightweight, hollow "beams" out of 1-by-4s or 1-by-6s as shown here. Assemble beams longer than 12 feet from multiple sections. Once assembled, the simulated beams can be finished in any number of decorative styles, from delicate hand-painted designs to a deliberately roughened surface.

Most simulated beams parallel each other across the width of a room and are hung from the existing joists. For a look that is more elaborate, add crossbeams at right angles between long beams. You can even erect posts along the walls beneath the ends of the beams and, as a final touch, attach bracing beams at 45-degree angles, running them from the posts to the ceiling beams.

 TOOLS

Circular saw
Hammer
Nail set
Block plane
Rasp
Electric drill with wire-brush attachment
Paintbrush
Electronic stud finder

 MATERIALS

Lumber (1 x 4s, 1 x 6s, 2 x 4s, 2 x 6s)
Carpenter's glue
Finishing nails (2")
Wood stain
Wood putty
Polyurethane finish
Sandpaper
Common nails ($3\frac{1}{2}$")
Toggle bolts

 SAFETY TIPS

Put on goggles when using a hammer. A hard hat offers good protection whenever there are unsecured boards overhead.

1. Building the beam.

◆ To make a hollow U-shaped beam, first measure and cut three 1-by-4s or 1-by-6s to the same length.
◆ Glue and nail the boards together with 2-inch finishing nails *(above)*, positioning the side pieces so that their edges overhang the bottom piece by no more than $\frac{1}{16}$ inch.
◆ Countersink the nails. Then plane the beam to make the bottom and lower edges of the sides flush with each other.
◆ Hold the beam temporarily in place against the ceiling to check its length before proceeding to Step 2.

112

2. Applying the finish.

To create a rough-hewn look, scrape the beam with a rasp *(left)*, scar it using a drill with a wire-brush attachment, or hit it with a chain or old keys; make sure to round and gouge the edges of the side pieces as you work. Apply a stain, then fill gaps and cover nailheads with matching wood putty.

To simulate a Tudor or Early American beam, bevel the edges of the side pieces and apply mahogany or walnut stain. Fill with matching wood putty and finish with polyurethane varnish.

For a beam with painted decorations, cover nailheads and fill gaps with wood putty. Sand the wood and add the design, with a stencil or freehand. Finish with polyurethane varnish.

3. Installing mounting tracks.

◆ For each beam made of 1-by-4s, cut a 2-by-4 of equal length. Use 2-by-6s for 1-by-6 beams.
◆ Locate ceiling joists with an electronic stud finder.
◆ With a helper, position each 2-by-4 or 2-by-6 as a

mounting track across the joists and fasten it to each with two $3\frac{1}{2}$-inch common nails *(above)*.

If the beams run parallel to and between joists, fasten the tracks to the ceiling with a toggle bolt every 2 feet.

4. Mounting a beam.

◆ With a helper, slide the beam onto its mounting track.
◆ Pressing the beam firmly against the ceiling, drive 2-inch finishing nails at 1-foot intervals through the sides of the beam and into the track. Countersink the nailheads.
◆ Cover the nailheads with matching wood putty and touch up the finish as needed.

Soundproofing a room can be tricky, because noise not only travels through air—directly and around corners—but also penetrates ordinary hollow walls with little loss of intensity.

Any vibrating surface—such as a loudspeaker cone or human vocal cords—starts air molecules moving in a wavelike pattern, transmitting acoustic energy to the eardrums. To be effective, a sound barrier must block airborne sound waves, interrupt acoustic energy transmitted through solids, and plug acoustic leaks. A solid brick wall is a good sound barrier, but the thin, flat surface of stud-and-wallboard construction is not. The flexible wallboard picks up sound vibrations and transmits them through the studs, setting in motion the wallboard on the other side.

The Tactic of Isolation: One way to weaken sound waves is to isolate a wall or ceiling surface from its supporting studs or joists, leaving at least 2 inches of space between surfaces. You can accomplish this when in-stalling new walls by mounting wallboard on resilient $\frac{1}{2}$-inch metal furring channels *(opposite)*. To add a sound-deadening layer over an existing wall, use 2-inch Z-shaped channels *(page 117)*.

Vibration is further reduced by leaving narrow gaps between adjacent wall surfaces and filling the gaps with flexible acoustic caulking compound that does not harden over time. You can suppress sound even more by filling the wall with fiberglass insulation; the fibers act like tiny springs to damp acoustic energy.

Sealing the Gaps: Holes and cracks in the wall can leak a surprising amount of noise. Plugging an opening $\frac{1}{8}$ inch wide around an electrical outlet box, for example, can improve the soundproofing effectiveness of a wall by as much as 10 percent. Other ways to suppress noise include damping vibrations in heating ducts and sealing gaps around doors *(page 121)*. Some central heating systems, however, may depend on gaps under interior doors for adequate air circulation.

 TOOLS

Tape measure
Plumb bob
Chalk line
Combination square

Power screwdriver
Staple gun
Framing hammer
Caulking gun
Electronic stud
   finder

 MATERIALS

Resilient furring
  channels
Z channels
Studs (2 x 4 and
  2 x 6)
Fiberglass insulation
Outlet box extender
Wallboard ($\frac{1}{2}$" and
  $\frac{5}{8}$")
Shims

Acoustic sealant
Nails (3" and $3\frac{1}{2}$")
Staples ($\frac{1}{2}$")
Neoprene-coated
  duct liner
Duct-liner adhesive
Door gasket
Threshold gasket
Dry-wall screws (1",
  $1\frac{1}{4}$", $1\frac{1}{2}$", and $1\frac{5}{8}$")
Brads
Wood screws (1")

 SAFETY TIPS

Wear a respirator, goggles, and gloves when removing plaster or wallboard and when handling fiberglass. Gloves are a must when handling resilient furring channels and Z channels, which are made of sheet metal.

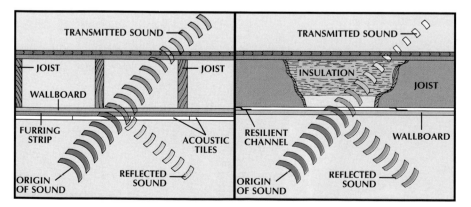

Sound absorption and transmission.
Porous acoustic tiles covering a wallboard ceiling *(far left)* reduce noise within a room by absorbing airborne sound waves, but they do a poor job of blocking sound transmission between rooms, since sound waves pass through their lightweight, porous composition. A wallboard ceiling that is mounted on resilient channels and that has insulation between the joists *(near left)* does little to suppress sound within a room, but it significantly reduces sound transmitted to the room above.

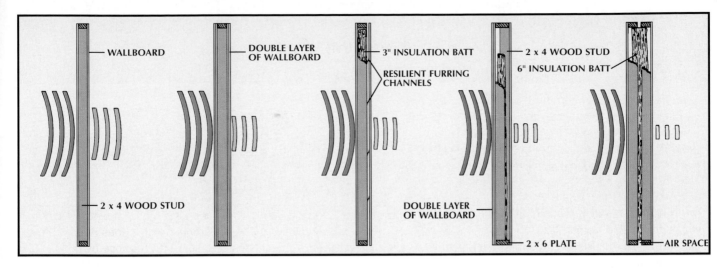

WALLBOARD

DOUBLE LAYER OF WALLBOARD

3" INSULATION BATT

RESILIENT FURRING CHANNELS

2 x 4 WOOD STUD

6" INSULATION BATT

2 x 4 WOOD STUD

DOUBLE LAYER OF WALLBOARD

2 x 6 PLATE

AIR SPACE

A variety of sound barriers.

The sound-reducing capabilities of the five walls diagramed above are determined by the thickness of the wall, the density and rigidity of the surface, and the nature of the contact between the surface and its support.

A standard 2-by-4 stud wall *(far left)* that is covered with one layer of wallboard renders conversation in the next room audible but indistinct.

A second layer of wallboard on each surface *(near left)* transmits only loud speech, but not clearly.

Mounting one layer of wallboard on resilient channels and adding a layer of insulation between studs *(center)* reduces sound transmission significantly.

Offsetting 2-by-4 studs on 2-by-6 plates, adding an insulation layer, and doubling one wallboard surface *(near right)* blocks both structural and airborne sound transmission dramatically.

Still more effective is the hollow double wall *(far right)*. With two pairs of 2-by-4 sole and top plates set 1 inch apart, a 6-inch layer of insulation, and a layer of wallboard on each side, this double wall stops sound better than a 4-inch solid brick wall.

SOUNDPROOFING AN EXISTING WALL

1. Attaching resilient furring channels.

◆ Remove the existing wall surface and pry out any nails.
◆ Add box extenders to electrical outlet boxes *(page 27)*, bringing their openings out $1\frac{1}{2}$ inches—$\frac{1}{2}$ inch for the channels and 1 inch for a double layer of $\frac{1}{2}$-inch wallboard.
◆ Staple $3\frac{1}{2}$-inch-thick batts of fiberglass insulation between studs.
◆ Snap a chalk line across the studs 6 inches below the ceiling and 2 inches above the floor. Between the lines, mark the studs for evenly spaced rows of channel 20 to 24 inches apart.
◆ Fasten the channel to the studs, mounting flange down, with $1\frac{1}{4}$-inch dry-wall screws driven through the holes provided in the flange. Position channel joints at studs, overlapping the channel sections at least 2 inches *(photograph)*.

⚠ **CAUTION** *When removing plaster or wallboard and when handling fiberglass, keep the room well ventilated. If you are demolishing a wall built before 1978, test for asbestos and lead (page 13).*

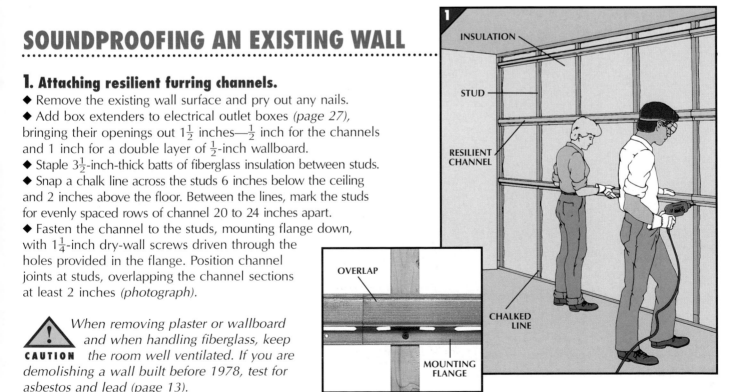

INSULATION

STUD

RESILIENT CHANNEL

CHALKED LINE

OVERLAP

MOUNTING FLANGE

2. Attaching the wallboard.

Install one layer of $\frac{1}{2}$-inch wallboard panels vertically, the second horizontally.

◆ Trim panels for the first layer $\frac{1}{4}$ inch shorter than the ceiling height.

◆ Shim the first panel to support it $\frac{1}{8}$ inch above the floor, then fasten it to the channels with 1-inch, fine-threaded dry-wall screws at 24-inch intervals.

◆ Remove the shims and use them to install the rest of the first layer, leaving a $\frac{1}{8}$-inch gap between panels.

◆ Caulk the gaps between panels and at the floor and ceiling with acoustic sealant *(inset)*.

◆ Install the second layer of wallboard, duplicating the $\frac{1}{8}$-inch gaps of the first. Use $1\frac{5}{8}$-inch dry-wall screws spaced 16 inches apart. Caulk the gaps with acoustic sealant.

◆ Complete the joints between panels and at the corners and ceiling with tape and joint compound, as shown on pages 34 to 37.

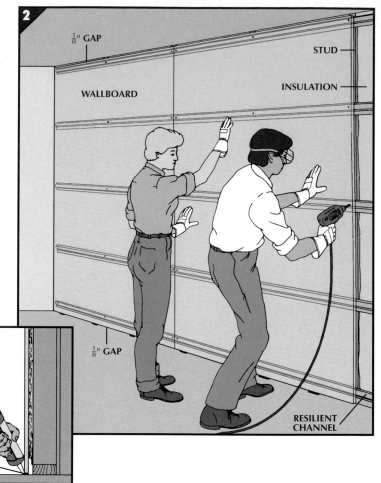

ACOUSTIC SEALANT

A FREESTANDING SOUND BUFFER

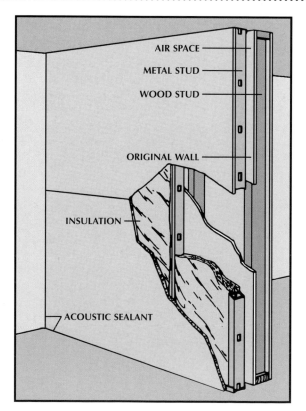

AIR SPACE
METAL STUD
WOOD STUD
ORIGINAL WALL
INSULATION
ACOUSTIC SEALANT

Cross section of a double wall.

A metal-stud wall constructed 2 inches away from an existing wall utilizes the space between walls and the inherent resiliency of metal studs as dual barriers to structure-borne sound. The wall is assembled as shown on pages 60 to 63 and covered with a single layer of $\frac{5}{8}$-inch wallboard. Spaces between studs are filled with $3\frac{1}{2}$-inch batts of fiberglass insulation to reduce airborne sound. Each panel of wallboard is installed $\frac{1}{8}$ inch away from adjacent surfaces, and the gaps are caulked with acoustic sealant.

This freestanding wall effectively suppresses the transmission of even low-pitched sounds, such as those produced by an electric bass guitar. You can further reduce noise transmission by removing the wallboard from the original wall to make room for additional insulation.

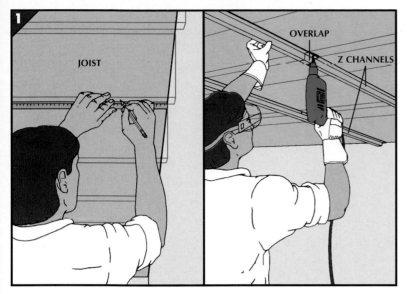

1. Attaching Z-shaped furring channels.

◆ Locate and mark joist positions as shown on page 22.

◆ Mark the ceiling 6 inches from both ends of the joists *(far left)*, then divide the space between the marks into equal intervals of 20 to 24 inches.

◆ Use the divisions to snap a series of chalked lines on the ceiling, perpendicular to the joists.

◆ Fasten the Z channels along the chalked lines with a $1\frac{1}{2}$-inch dry-wall screw at each joist *(near left)*, making sure that all the flanged edges face in the same direction. When joining lengths of channel, overlap the ends 2 inches and fasten them to the joist with a single screw.

2. Adding wallboard and insulation.

Start mounting the wallboard panels at the side of the room opposite to the direction the open flange is pointing.

◆ Mount the first row of wallboard to the Z channels, using 1-inch, fine-threaded dry-wall screws at 12-inch intervals and leaving a $\frac{1}{8}$-inch gap between the panel edges and adjacent walls. If more than one panel is needed to span the ceiling, center the joint between panels on the lower flange of the metal channel *(inset)*. Drive the screw nearest the flange corner first, to prevent the flange from sagging and ensure a smooth seam between panels.

◆ After installing the first row of panels, insert 2-inch-thick batts of fiberglass insulation on top of the wallboard between the joists.

◆ Install additional rows of wallboard and insulation as above, with the exception of the last row. There, glue the insulation batt to the back of the panel before fastening it to the channels.

◆ Caulk all of the $\frac{1}{8}$-inch gaps with acoustic sealant. Finish the seams between panels with tape and joint compound, as shown on pages 34 to 37.

REBUILDING A CEILING

1. Creating space for insulation.
◆ Uncover the ceiling joists, observing the same precautions as in removing a wall *(page 13)*. Pry out any nails that remain in the joists.
◆ If the room has a ceiling light fixture, extend the electrical outlet box *(page 27, bottom)*.
◆ Install 6-inch-thick batts of fiberglass insulation between the exposed joists and against the subfloor above. Staple the batts to the sides of the joists at 2- to 3-inch intervals.

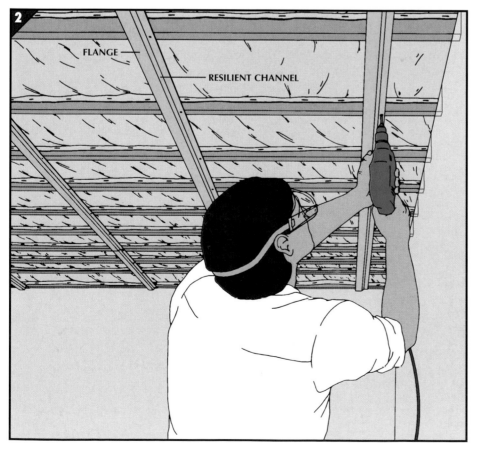

FLANGE

RESILIENT CHANNEL

2. Attaching resilient channels.
Install resilient furring channels across the exposed joists, following the method for Z channels shown on page 117, Step 1. Make sure all the flanges face the same direction. Plan channel joints to fall at joists and overlap the sections at least 2 inches.

◆ Fasten wallboard panels across the resilient channels using 1-inch drywall screws, leaving a $\frac{1}{8}$-inch gap around the perimeter of the ceiling. Center joints between panels on channel flanges and fasten the panels as shown on page 116, Step 2.
◆ Caulk all the gaps with an acoustic sealant, and finish the seams between panels as described on pages 34 to 37.

OFFSET STUDS TO MUFFLE SOUND

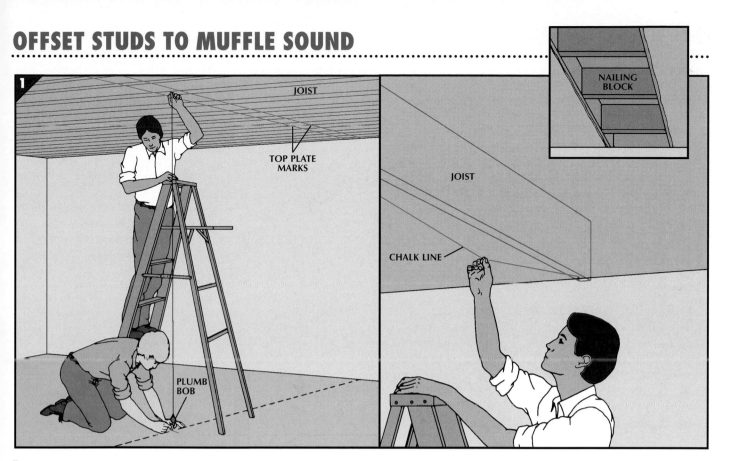

JOIST

TOP PLATE MARKS

PLUMB BOB

JOIST

CHALK LINE

NAILING BLOCK

1. Locating the top and sole plates.

This sound-resistant wall requires top and bottom plates of 2-by-6s instead of the 2-by-4s used for most walls. For a wall running perpendicular to joists *(above, left)*, snap two parallel chalked lines across the ceiling $5\frac{1}{2}$ inches apart. Drop a plumb bob near the ends of each line, mark the floor, and snap guidelines for the sole plate.

To build a wall parallel to joists, center the top plate directly under a joist if possible *(above, right)*.
◆ Locate the joist with a stud finder *(page 8)*. Then, at each side of the room, drive a nail partway into the joist at the centerline.
◆ Snap a chalk line between the two nails to mark the centerline of the top plate, then snap the chalk line $2\frac{3}{4}$ inches from the centerline on either side to outline the top plate.
◆ Duplicate the lines on the floor for the sole plate, as described above.

If the wall must stand between joists, expose the two joists that will flank the new wall, and install nailing blocks of joist lumber between them *(inset)*. Toenail a block every 2 feet and fill between them with insulation. Then patch the ceiling *(pages 34-37)* and snap chalked lines for the plates as if the wall were running perpendicular to the joists.

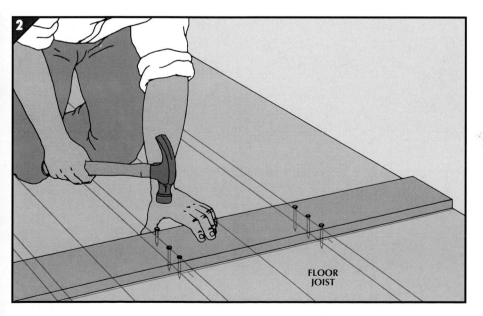

FLOOR JOIST

2. Installing the sole plate.
◆ Cut 2-by-6 lumber to the length of the wall for both the sole plate and the top plate.
◆ For a wall perpendicular to joists, find the joists with a stud finder and mark their centers along one side of the outline.
◆ Set the 2-by-6 sole plate within the outline and fasten it to the underlying joists with $3\frac{1}{2}$-inch nails *(left)*.

If the new wall runs parallel to the joists, simply nail the sole plate to the floor, driving $3\frac{1}{2}$-inch nails at 16-inch intervals.

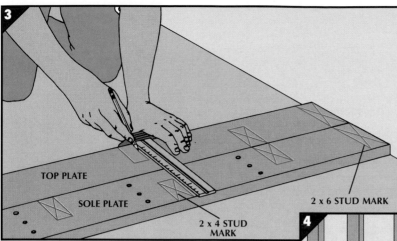

TOP PLATE

SOLE PLATE

2 x 4 STUD MARK

2 x 6 STUD MARK

3. Marking the plates for studs.
◆ Mark each end of the sole plate for a 2-by-6 stud.
◆ Next, mark the sole plate every 12 inches for a 2-by-4 stud. Align the first stud with one edge of the sole plate, the second stud with the other edge, and so on.
◆ Lay the top plate beside the sole plate and, using a combination square, transfer the marks to the top plate as shown at left.

4. Assembling the framework.
◆ With one or more helpers, fasten the top plate to the ceiling as planned in Step 1 on page 119. Use $3\frac{1}{2}$-inch nails.
◆ Measure the distance between the sole and top plates, and cut two 2-by-6 studs to this length. Nail them to the ends of the plates—and to the adjacent walls, but only if there is a stud in the existing wall to nail to.
◆ Cut 2-by-4 studs to fit between the plates and align them with the marks on the top and sole plate. Toenail them in place with 3-inch nails, two nails on one side, a third on the other.

5. Completing the wall.
◆ Fasten batts of fiberglass insulation, $3\frac{1}{2}$ inches thick and 24 inches wide, between the studs, using $\frac{1}{2}$-inch staples to hold the batts in place.
◆ Cover both sides of the wall with a double layer of $\frac{1}{2}$-inch wallboard, staggering joints and leaving a $\frac{1}{8}$-inch gap around the edges of the wall.
◆ Caulk the $\frac{1}{8}$-inch gaps on both sides of the wall with acoustic sealant. Finish wallboard joints with tape and joint compound as shown on pages 34 to 37.

A DOUBLE WALL TO STOP LOW-PITCHED SOUND

Constructing the two walls.
◆ Mark the floor and ceiling for two 2-by-4 sole plates and two top plates, 1 inch apart. Cut the plates, set them side by side, and mark them for 2-by-4 studs, 16 inches on center.
◆ Assemble the frames as shown at left, toenailing the studs to the plates.
◆ Staple 6-inch-thick batts of fiberglass insulation between the studs.
◆ Cover the outer wall surfaces with a double layer of $\frac{1}{2}$-inch wallboard, staggering joints and leaving $\frac{1}{8}$-inch gaps around the edges.
◆ Caulk perimeter gaps with acoustic sealant and finish seams with tape and joint compound *(pages 34-37)*.

PLUGGING ACOUSTIC LEAKS

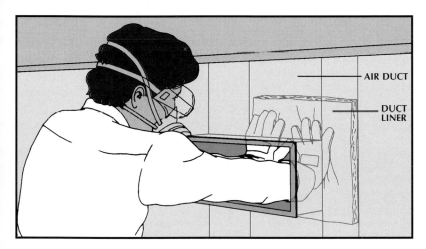

Muffling an air duct.
◆ Remove the register and measure as far into the duct as your arms will reach in both directions.
◆ Cut three pieces of 1-inch-thick neoprene-coated fiberglass duct liner to this length and wide enough to fit snugly along the back and sides of the duct, without blocking the register.
◆ Seal the cut edges of the pieces with duct-liner adhesive to prevent glass fibers from being released into the air.
◆ Working with one piece of liner at a time, spread duct-liner adhesive on the rough, uncoated side of each piece and press it into place on the duct wall.
◆ Replace the register.

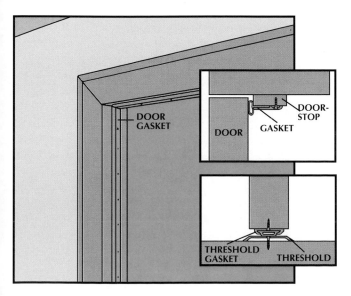

Sealing interior doors.
◆ Cut lengths of vinyl weatherproofing gasket to fit along the stops at the top and sides of the doorframe *(upper inset)*. Test-fit the gasket by holding it against the frame and closing the door; the gasket should compress slightly without interfering with the latch.
◆ Attach the gasket to the stops with 1-inch brads at 3-inch intervals. If the gasket has a metal mounting strip, you may substitute 1-inch wood screws for the brads.
◆ Measure the gap between the bottom of the door and the threshold; if the doorframe has no threshold, install one made of either aluminum or wood.
◆ Remove the door from the frame and trim the bottom of the door to accommodate a threshold gasket mounted in a metal strip *(lower inset)*. Install the gasket with 1-inch wood screws.
◆ Rehang the door and test the gasket fit by sliding a credit card between the gasket and the threshold; the card should meet slight resistance.

121

The nooks and crannies within the framework of a conventional house can be handy places to store or hide items not so valuable as to be better off in a safe-deposit box. For instance, bookshelves, seemingly as immobile as the wall to which they are attached, can swing open to reveal a set of shelves, or a closet ceiling can tilt up to disclose an unsuspected recess.

Choosing the Right Place: The location of such hiding places must naturally be limited to interior wall areas that are free of ducts, wires, or pipes, but it is not necessarily restricted in size to the standard $3\frac{1}{2}$-inch thickness of a stud wall. If you can mount bookshelves on a wall that is located beneath a staircase, or against a wall with a closet on the far side, you can have a secret storage area of considerable size.

Bookshelf Requirements: Swinging bookshelves must be strong. Build them of lumber at least $\frac{3}{4}$ inch thick; joints must be rabbeted. In addition, the shelves need a plywood back and a 1-by-2 horizontal brace along the inside where the back meets the top.

Mount the bookshelves on the wall with special hardware called pivot hinges, which are nearly but not completely invisible; choose a height for the shelves so that hinges are above and below eye level. Although pivot hinges are made in sizes that will support as much as 150 pounds, keep weight on the bookshelves to a minimum, reserving them for knickknacks and photographs rather than heavy books.

TOOLS

Wood chisel
Mallet
Screwdriver
Hammer
Miter box and
  backsaw
Block plane

MATERIALS

Plywood ($\frac{1}{4}$")
1 x 2s
1 x 4s
Finishing nails (1",
  $1\frac{1}{2}$", 2", $2\frac{1}{2}$")
Spackling compound or
  adhesive joint tape
Contact cement
Pivot hinges with
  screws
Thin strips of wood,
  felt, or rubber
Door or window
  molding ($\frac{3}{8}$")
Spring-action catch
Wallboard
Wallboard adhesive
Joint compound
Cove molding

SAFETY TIPS

Protect your eyes with goggles when driving nails with a hammer or when working with a drill.

A HIDDEN RECESS BEHIND A BOOKCASE

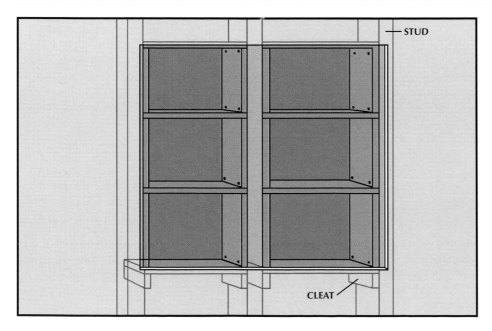

STUD

CLEAT

Creating recessed shelves.

This wall opening, made by cutting away wallboard or plaster and lath, stretches between the centers of two studs, 32 inches apart. Shelves are made from 1-by-4s that fit flush with stud edges. The bottom shelves rest on 1-by-2 cleats. Lengths of 1-by-4 attached to the sides of studs with finishing nails serve as supports for the two middle shelves. At the top of each shelf unit a board the same size as a shelf is nailed to its supports to form an inverted U, which is then slipped into place and nailed to the studs. The wallboard edge around the opening is smoothed with spackling compound or adhesive joint tape.

HOW TO SUSPEND THE BOOKCASE

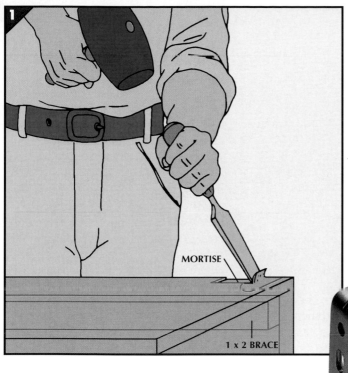

MORTISE

1 x 2 BRACE

1. Mortising for the hinges.

◆ Outline the bookshelf leaf of a pivot hinge *(photograph)* on the top of the shelves, positioning the hinge $\frac{1}{4}$ inch from the side of the unit.

◆ With a wood chisel and mallet, cut a mortise as deep as the thickness of the hinge *(left)*. Do the same at the bottom of the unit.

◆ With the screws provided by the manufacturer, fasten both hinges to the back of the unit through the elongated holes.

◆ Have a helper hold the shelves in position at the side of the opening. On the stud edge there, outline each stud-leaf hinge and mark screw hole positions.

◆ Unscrew the hinges from the shelves and, using the outlines as guides, fasten the hinges to the stud through the elongated holes.

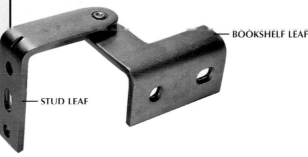

BOOKSHELF LEAF

STUD LEAF

STUD

WALLBOARD

PIVOT HINGE

BOOKSHELVES

2. Mounting the unit.

◆ While a helper holds the shelf unit against the stud, adjust the positions of the hinges, then drive screws through all the holes in both stud leaves.

◆ Mount the shelves on the hinges with screws driven through the elongated holes in the bookshelf leaf.

◆ Open and close the unit to check for proper action of the hinges *(inset)*, making adjustments as necessary.

◆ When the shelves close neatly against the recess, drive screws through all the remaining holes in the hinges.

◆ With contact cement, attach thin strips of wood, felt, or rubber to the stud against which the shelves close, so that the unit protrudes equally from the studs on both sides.

3. Disguising the joint with molding.

◆ Miter four sections of $\frac{3}{8}$-inch door or window molding to frame the recess, then notch the top and bottom sections to fit around the hinges.

◆ Tack the molding around the recess and close the shelf unit. If it rubs the molding, shave the unit's edges with a block plane until it slips snugly into the frame. Move the molding only if its alignment is obviously wrong, in order to avoid leaving a visible gap between the molding and the bookshelves when the unit is closed.

◆ Nail the molding to the wall.

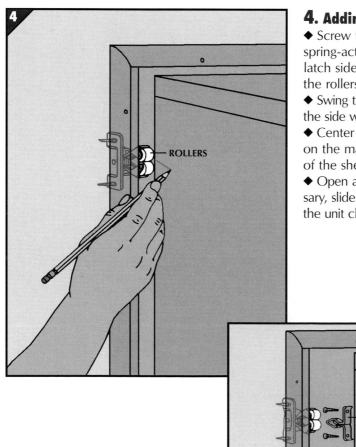

ROLLERS

LATCH

4. Adding a catch.

◆ Screw the double-roller half of a spring-action catch to the stud at the latch side of the opening, positioning the rollers flush with the stud edge.

◆ Swing the unit nearly closed and mark the side where the two rollers meet.

◆ Center the latching half of the catch on the mark and screw it to the back of the shelf unit (inset).

◆ Open and close the shelves. If necessary, slide the rollers in or out to hold the unit closed tightly against the wall.

A FALSE CEILING IN A CLOSET

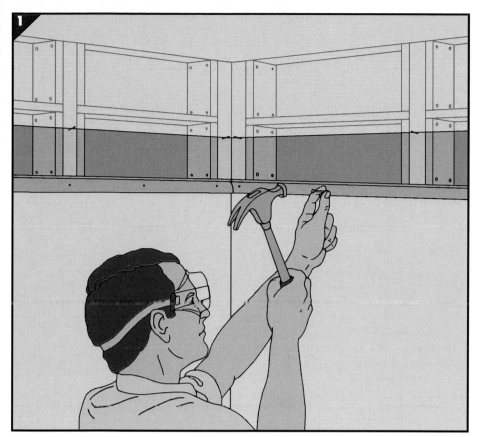

1. Attaching the molding.
◆ At least 4 inches above the molding on the top of the closet door construct a storage area as on page 122.

◆ Cut a piece of wallboard and a piece of $\frac{1}{4}$-inch plywood $\frac{1}{2}$ inch smaller than the dimensions of the closet. Nail the wallboard to the plywood with 1-inch finishing nails spaced every 6 inches along the edge. Cover the nailheads with joint compound *(page 34)*.

◆ Raise the wallboard panel several inches above the bottom shelf and rest it temporarily on $2\frac{1}{2}$-inch finishing nails tapped into the studs.

◆ Cut mitered lengths of small cove molding to fit the perimeter of the closet and attach it to the wall at the desired height with wallboard adhesive and 2-inch finishing nails. Hammer the nails through the concave section of the molding into the studs, including those at the corners.

◆ Drive nails at a slight angle into the wallboard between studs to hold the molding while the adhesive sets.

2. Installing the false ceiling.
Remove the finishing nails supporting the wallboard panel and lower it onto the molding. To access the shelves, tilt up the panel.

INDEX

Time-Life Books is a division of Time Life Inc.

PRESIDENT and CEO: John M. Fahey Jr.

TIME-LIFE BOOKS

MANAGING EDITOR: Roberta Conlan

Director of Design: Michael Hentges
Editorial Production Manager:
  Ellen Robling
Director of Operations: Eileen Bradley
Director of Photography and Research:
  John Conrad Weiser
Senior Editors: Russell B. Adams Jr.,
  Janet Cave, Lee Hassig, Robert
  Somerville, Henry Woodhead
Library: Louise D. Forstall

PRESIDENT: John D. Hall

*Vice President, Director of New Product
  Development:* Neil Kagan
*Associate Director, New Product
  Development:* Quentin S. McAndrew
Marketing Director: James Gillespie
Vice President, Book Production:
  Marjann Caldwell
Production Manager: Marlene Zack
Quality Assurance Manager: James King

HOME REPAIR AND IMPROVEMENT

SERIES EDITOR: Lee Hassig
Administrative Editor: Barbara Levitt

Editorial Staff for *Walls and Ceilings*
Senior Art Director: Cynthia Richardson
Picture Editor: Catherine Chase Tyson
Text Editors: Denise Dersin, Glen Ruh
Associate Editors/Research-Writing:
  Terrell Smith, Jarelle Stein
Copyeditor: Judith Klein
Picture Coordinator: Paige Henke
Editorial Assistant: Amy S. Crutchfield

Special Contributors: John Drummond
  (illustration); Jennifer Gearhart, Marvin
  Shultz, Eileen Wentland (digital illustration); George Constable (text); Mel
  Ingber (index).

Correspondents: Christine Hinze (London),
  Christina Lieberman (New York), Maria
  Vincenza Aloisi (Paris).

PICTURE CREDITS

Cover: Photograph, Renée Comet. Art,
  Peter J. Malamas/Totally Incorporated.

Illustrators: Jack Arthur, Frederic F. Bigio from
B-C Graphics, Lazlo Bodrogi, Roger Essley,
Charles Forsythe, Adisai Hemintranont from
Sai Graphis, Elsie Hennig, Walter Hilmers Jr.
from HJ Commercial Art, Dick Lee, John
Martinez, John Massey, Joan S. McGurren,
W. F. McWilliam, Eduino J. Pereira, Ray
Skibinski, Snowden Associates, Inc.

Photographers: **End papers:** Renée Comet.
8: Renée Comet. **9:** Trus Joist MacMillan;
Southern Pine Council. **11:** Renée
Comet. **21:** Porter-Cable Professional
Power Tools. **29:** Renée Comet (2).
31: PANELLIFT® brand dry-wall lift man-
ufactured by Telpro Inc. **35, 36, 37, 45,
46, 48:** Renée Comet. **53:** Design Brick
Products. **57:** Renée Comet, prop courtesy the Door Store, Washington, D.C.
61, 63, 73, 79, 82, 95, 104, 105: Renée
Comet. **108:** Laser Tools Company.
115, 123: Renée Comet, hinge #327
courtesy Stanley Hardware.

ACKNOWLEDGMENTS

Esther del Rosario, Washington, D.C.; Steve
Francis, American Brick Company, Detroit;
John Hollern, Dodge-Regupol, Inc., Lan-
caster, Pa.; Todd Langston, Porter-Cable
Power Tools, Jackson, Tenn.; David Marlin-
ski, Morristown, N.J.; David Stone, Styleline
Systems Division of Daston, Inc., Wal-
worth, Wis.; Bill West, Metropolitan Rolling
Door, Inc., Columbia, Md.

**Library of Congress
Cataloging-in-Publication Data**
Walls and ceilings / by the editors of Time-
  Life Books.
  p. cm. — (Home repair and improvement)
Includes index.
ISBN 0-7835-3900-2
1. Interior walls—Amateurs' manuals.
  2. Ceilings—Amateurs' manuals.
  3. Dwellings—Remodeling—Amateurs'
  manuals.
I. Time-Life Books. II. Series.
TH2239.T55 1996
643'.7—dc20   95-49608